THE JUDAS FACTOR

THE JUDAS FACTOR

DWIGHT JONES

CREATION
HOUSE

THE JUDAS FACTOR by Dwight Jones
Published by Creation House
A Charisma Media Company
600 Rinehart Road
Lake Mary, Florida 32746
www.charismamedia.com

Unless otherwise noted, all Scripture quotations are from King James Version.

Scripture quotations marked NKJV are taken from the New King James Version®. Copyright © 1982 by Thomas Nelson. Used by permission. All rights reserved.

Scripture quotations marked GW are taken from GOD'S WORD®, © 1995 God's Word to the Nations. Used by permission of Baker Publishing Group. All rights reserved.

Scripture quotations marked NIV are taken from the Holy Bible, New International Version®, NIV®. Copyright © 1973, 1978, 1984, 2011 by Biblica, Inc.™ Used by permission of Zondervan. All rights reserved worldwide. www.zondervan.com The "NIV" and "New International Version" are trademarks registered in the United States Patent and Trademark Office by Biblica, Inc.™

Scripture quotations marked NLT are from the Holy Bible, New Living Translation, copyright © 1996, 2004, 2007. Used by permission of Tyndale House Publishers, Inc., Wheaton, IL 60189. All rights reserved.

Design Director: Justin Evans
Cover design by Justin Evans

Visit the author's website: www.DwightJonesMinistries.org

Library of Congress Cataloging-in-Publication Data:
2015952365
International Standard Book Number: 978-1-62998-500-8
E-book International Standard Book Number:
978-1-62998-501-5

While the author has made every effort to provide accurate telephone numbers and Internet addresses at the time of publication, neither the publisher nor the author assumes any responsibility for errors or for changes that occur after publication.

First edition

15 16 17 18 19 — 987654321
Printed in Canada

TABLE OF CONTENTS

FOREWORD

I AM AMAZED AT the revelation knowledge coming to light in our generation. Phenomenal truths, tucked away through the ages, as well as ancient mysteries, are now coming to light. Knowledge is increasing at an exponential rate; likewise, supernatural revelation is increasing. I have to admit that it is difficult at times to keep up. I regularly pick up books—and just by glancing through them, I can barely put them down. Page after page captures my attention to the point that I often wonder why I have not seen these truths before. I believe the Holy Spirit is revealing them to studious and diligent Word people, arming us for the days ahead.

From the time I saw the title, *The Judas Factor*, this book caught my eye. I knew that the author, Dwight Jones, was on to something. It was difficult to put the book aside because I knew there had to be an anointing on the author to come up with such insight. There is no doubt about it: The end times are no longer coming; they are here right now. We must face this fact. Signs are everywhere, and they are screaming at a lost and dying world that the coming of our Lord Jesus Christ is at hand.

As His coming draws closer, we need to remember that the heart is a very difficult thing to know. Increasingly, it is going to be the issue in the days to come. As a matter of fact, the Lord asks who can know it; it is deceptive and wicked (Jer. 17:9). The same sun that melts wax hardens clay. May we always remain tender before Him.

Even though Peter denied the Lord, Judas betrayed Him, and there is a vast difference between the two. I see a trend today of many denying out of fear, but betrayal is something much more sinister; and it is the result of a spiritual issue. Judas was not able to find redemption for betraying innocent blood. Will America? The parallels of the closing hours of Jesus' earthly life, and the plot that unfolded as the betrayer became apostate, should move us to begin to ask, "Lord, is it I?" America is on the brink of disaster—one that can only be diverted by repentance.

Dwight Jones is sounding an alarm. He writes with passion and persuasion and is shining a bright light on a dark subject. He does it with accuracy as he sounds a clarion call for repentance. I believe he has been given this word for this hour and that laity and pulpits alike must heed the call. As you read this book, don't just go through it; allow it to go through you.

—John A. Kilpatrick
Founder and Senior Pastor
Church of His Presence
Daphne, Alabama

INTRODUCTION

The Judas Factor

A S A STUDENT and preacher of eschatology (Bible prophecy), I have spoken much about America and the role she will likely play in the end-time scenario. I am a firm believer that America is fading quickly from her perch atop the world and will not be a major player in end-time events.

We have a president and leadership that are seemingly bent on destroying this nation, and they are doing a very good job of it. We have rejected the God of the Bible and embraced Allah, the god of Islam. We are slaughtering thousands of babies every day in our government-funded abortion clinics. We are a nation at war. Race wars and riots fill our streets as businesses are burned and police officers are criminalized. There is an unholy alliance between the White House and the Supreme Court to systematically unravel the fabric of our society.

We watch as thousands of Christians are martyred, women are raped, and children beheaded or forced into human trafficking—and we seem to be unable to respond. As we have accepted Allah and the religion of Islam, we must by necessity reject Jehovah and the Judeo-Christian way of life because no one can serve two masters. We have

xi

[handwritten: from carter → to now]

[handwritten: Complete all at once]

watched our president drive a wedge between us and Israel. We have distanced ourselves from Israel and are attempting to forge a covenant with their sworn enemy, Iran.

Recently as I was praying for America and for a great awakening, I prayed a very simple prayer. It was as follows:

Father, please judge our leadership, but spare our nation.

[handwritten: Wow!]

I don't know what I expected as a response or if I expected one at all, but I received one and it floored me. I heard the Lord speak to me these words: "I cannot do that. *[handwritten: ✱]* I cannot judge the leader and spare the people, for to do so would be to act contrary to My word. I must judge those equally, for it was the people who chose the leader."

What did these words mean, and what was the judgment that He would bring? Would it be calamity? Would it be another terrorist attack? What was the form that this coming judgment would take? For the next couple of weeks I sought the Lord for clarity. If judgment was coming, and I firmly believed it was, what did that portend for the church?

Like the sons of Issachar in the Bible, I longed to know what was coming down the pipe. While I was meditating on the many things that were unfolding in the prophetic realm, God spoke to me with some of the most sobering words that I have ever heard: "As Judas betrayed Christ with a kiss and sold him to His enemies, so America will betray Israel and sell her to her enemies!" There was no mistaking what I had just heard. This was a warning to America, and I was shaken to say the least.

America has been blessed by God, and His blessings upon this nation have set it apart from all others. He said he would bless those who bless Israel, but He also has promised a curse to those who curse Israel. He pronounced a dire warning to the nations in Joel 3:2. God said He would bring those nations who have divided His land to the valley of Jehoshaphat and judge them there.

Now my prayer had taken a new direction, I knew what America was going to do—but what did that mean for the church? It was from that prayer and the ensuing revelation that I write this book.

We, the church, are not without hope. God has us in the palm of His hand, and He has promised to be faithful to us. We must, however, repent and return to our first love. We must find a secret place with Him where we die to selfish ambition and self-centered desires for "crowds and crowns."

When we do, we will come out of hiding and walk in the power of God. We will see a repairing of the breach, and we will be restorers of His path (Isa. 58:12). We will see many modern-day pillow prophets humbled and repent before God. We will also see many others who will continue to go down the road of betrayal. However, God will raise the church out of the ashes, and as the Lord said through His Prophet Joel and again through Peter on the Day of Pentecost, "I will pour out of My Spirit in those days" (see Joel 2:28–29; Acts 2:17–18). No one and nothing can stop Him. The only thing you have to decide is which side you will stand on.

CHAPTER 1

THE LAST DAYS SCENARIO

JESUS

IT WAS VERY early Thursday morning when the sun began to rise over the sleeping masses gathered in Jerusalem on that spring day. This was no ordinary day; this was the morning before Passover was to begin. In a few, short hours the streets of this Holy City would be teeming with people as they made their final preparations for this most sacred celebration. The past week had brought with it more emotions than one could begin to process. Only days earlier, Jesus had ridden into town to one of the greatest scenes described in Scripture. The King of kings had been welcomed by the throngs of people as they shouted, "Hosanna in the highest!" Palm branches had been laid in the streets, and songs filled the air as He came riding in on the back of a donkey. But that was then, and so much had happened since that not-so-distant day.

Jerusalem was beginning to wake up. Shopkeepers began to stir as they prepared their wares for this shortened workday. Noise filled the streets as people by the thousands began making their final preparations for Passover. The room was to be secured where Jesus and the disciples would gather together, and everything had to be just right. This was the day the Lord had spoken about for more than three years; indeed, this was the day for which He was born. This would be the greatest Passover celebration Israel would ever experience. This would be His last Passover with them. Their last sacrifice was about to be led as a lamb to the slaughter.

In the garden in the early days of His ministry, Jesus told Nicodemus of the love of the Father—so great that He would send His one and only Son as a ransom for the entire world. He had tried to prepare them for what was coming. Jesus was, as John said, "the Lamb of God," and everyone knew the purpose of the Lamb (John 1:29, 36).

He told them that there was coming a day when the "Bridegroom would be taken from them" (Luke 5:35). He warned them that "as Jonah was three days in the whale's belly; so shall the Son of man be three days and three nights in the heart of the earth" (Matt. 12:40). Often Christ had said that He would give His life to bring life to the world. Jesus of Nazareth was "the good shepherd... [who] giveth his life for the sheep," and the "heir whom the evil husbandmen cast out and killed" (see John 10:11; Luke 20:9–16). They had to know that this was His purpose, this was His day, and it was moving way too quickly.

The afternoon sun was beginning its descent over the mountains of Jerusalem. The busy streets became silent as the crowds gathered in houses all over the city to celebrate Passover. As the evening drew near, Jesus and His disciples sat down to eat and to remember the day when the blood of the lamb was shed to protect Israel from death in Egypt. In a few short hours, the Lamb would give His life once and for all.

ISRAEL, GOD'S TIMEPIECE

In the fourth chapter of Deuteronomy, Moses prophesied to the nation of Israel. He said there was coming a day when Israel would be scattered to the nations of the world. He also said that in the "latter days" they would be drawn back to their promised land. Indeed, Israel had been scattered from one end of the Earth to the other. The Holy City had been laid waste, and the people were, as Moses had said, "few in number" (Deut. 4:27).

Adolf Hitler and his demonic Third Reich attempted the unthinkable; they tried to remove them from the earth. The Jewish people had survived the ovens of Auschwitz and the other 1500 concentration camps, and they were now returning to their homeland. It was as Ezekiel the prophet had said; "an exceeding great army" had risen from the bone yard (Ezek. 37:10). This army was being gathered from the four corners of the Earth, and they were now coming to the very place that God had promised Abraham He would give them.

The "times of the Gentiles" is quickly drawing to a close (Luke 21:24). Benjamin Netanyahu, the Prime Minister of Israel, has said on many occasions, "Israel's enemies must know, whatever the cost, even if we have to *stand alone*... Israel is our eternal homeland and Jerusalem was and always will be our capital. There will never be another holocaust."[1]

Stand alone? Would Israel ever have to really stand alone? God has warned Israel that they would be turned upon by every nation, and now it seems that time has come. We are seeing the fulfillment of that prophecy as

3

Are we really so? [handwritten]

America, Israel's best friend and staunchest supporter, now distances herself from the people of God.

JUDAS

Judas Iscariot. His name is self-descriptive; he was "the traitor." He was one of the twelve disciples of Jesus, but oh so much more than that—he was "the treasurer." He carried the purse; he handled the finances for the greatest ministry team in history. That Thursday morning was different from any he had experienced. On this day, the wheels of his mind were turning fast; he wondered how it would all play out and why it was taking so long. He had been up before sunrise; he couldn't sleep, not now. This was his time, and this day seemed to be moving ever so slowly. Something, indeed someone, was driving him. He had a task to accomplish, and that task must not be impeded.

There were meetings to attend, important meetings. Today he was going to pull the proverbial trigger. Sure, he would have to go through the motions of his job as treasurer, but today he was going to make a name for himself. Everyone would know who Judas Iscariot was. He would establish his legacy, and what a legacy it would be!

The sun was up and now brightly shining over Jerusalem; evening couldn't get here soon enough. He wanted to get this thing over with. He had accepted the task and was ready to "change the world"—and none dare interfere. The day had been long, but finally the evening shadows began to deepen. Tonight history would be made, and he would seal it with a kiss...

AMERICA

We now stand at a crossroad in America as our leadership has begun to distance itself from Israel. Something has changed in this once powerful relationship. What has happened? Why are they so determined to appease the enemy, even to the point of selling out their staunchest ally? Would the United States of America turn her back on Israel at such a crucial moment in history?

There have been only 44 presidents in this nation's brief but illustrious history. The United States of America, that "shining city on a hill," was founded upon the principles of the Word of God and raised from obscurity. Now America stands as the sole superpower of the world. From the dark night of the revolution to the horror of a civil war that claimed more than 600,000 lives, this nation is a nation of destiny. She survived World War I and the Great Depression, along with World War II, and the Korean and Vietnam conflicts. America seems to be unstoppable.

We stood strong against our enemies both at home and abroad. The blight of slavery long removed from our homeland, we were a nation to be reckoned with. It was the time for "hope and change," and what a change there would be! It was time to truly shine. It was time for the world to see a new America, one that would be fundamentally changed. This was a new day; our enemies needed to see that we were different.

Barack Hussein Obama's day had come! In June of 2009, he told Benjamin Netanyahu, "We are going to change the world, so don't interfere."[2] This was the hour of Barack Obama, and he would be sure to make the most of it. There was a legacy to be established, and at home that legacy would be easy enough. His minions in the House and Senate, along with his friends in the liberal media, would push his agenda through. "Healthcare for all Americans"—done! The demolition of our economy—accomplished! He was even able to destroy the institution of marriage.

However, his legacy internationally was a bit more difficult. There was a task that no one before him had been able to accomplish, but he was different. Peace in the Middle East was the goal, and the only way to make it happen was to solve this Israeli / Palestinian problem.

There were meetings that needed to take place if this Israeli thing was going to be solved in his presidency. "Changing the world"—what a noble thought! It was a daunting task, but "Allah willing," as Mr. Kerry said, "It was possible." If there was to be peace in the Middle East, Iran would need to be on board. Thanks to Mr. Obama's connections through an Iranian insider in his government by the name of Ms. Valerie Jarrett, even that might be accomplished.

If achieving peace is the goal, then there would have to be concessions on everyone's part. If the long-lasting relationship with Israel is a casualty of the negotiations, then so be it. With the deal all but done, the sun is beginning to set on America.

THE DISCIPLES

What a week! Can you imagine the crowds screaming and shouting "Hosanna" as Jesus and His followers entered Jerusalem? Can you imagine the excitement in the hearts of the disciples? "There must have been a million people there!" They wondered, "When is Jesus going to set up His kingdom? What position will we have in it?" There was something different in the atmosphere. It was a strange feeling, but what was it?

Thursday morning had come, and the streets were crowded. Everyone was trying to tie up loose ends as they prepared for Passover. Jesus had told the disciples to get things ready, and they were up to the task. There was a kingdom to be established, and this might just be the culmination of the three years of preparation.

This Jesus they had walked with was indeed the Son of God! He was the Messiah, and they knew it! Everyone knew it, didn't they? I mean, just a few days ago it seemed like all of Israel had welcomed him and shouted, "Blessed is He who comes in the name of the Lord!" You don't get more Messianic than that. He was the Messiah, and they were His chosen disciples.

This was their hour, and although some had forsaken Jesus, they were in it forever. Indeed, they had made that clear to Him time and again. The disciples had watched the crowds come and go, but their commitment to him was resolute: "We will never leave You, Lord."

It would be evening soon, and everything had to be just right. This was Passover, and it couldn't get here soon enough...

THE CHURCH!

What a powerful name we have been given! To think that God in His sovereignty, with the ability to place us at any point in time, at any place in history, chose to make us part of the church in these last days. The hour that we are living in was desired by all of the prophets. The closing moments of time are upon us. This is our destiny! We are nearly two billion strong, and our influence is one to be

U.S. is NOT 2 Billion.

reckoned with. We have mega churches and name recognition. We are unstoppable. We have been brought to the kingdom for such a time as this.

There is a job to be done, and we have the best and brightest minds working on the task. Sure, we have had to change some things and shed some of those old ways of doing things, but this isn't our grandma's church—this is a new day. Those old traditions had to go. We will never fulfill our mandate with those old wineskins. It is time to put aside divisive matters and find a way to let the masses know who we are. We are not here to offend anyone; that's out of style.

We have changed both the messages that are preached and the way we deliver them. We are the new and improved church. There are some who don't want to acquiesce. They're always preaching about holiness and revival and "the end times." Why can't those "old fashioned" preachers understand that "the wealth of the wicked has been laid up for us"?

The modern church doesn't have time to worry about the end times. The modern pastors seem to be more focused on the societal needs rather than the eternal ones. The focus of the church is crowds and crowns. The message of the Cross is outdated and out of sync. The opinion of many within the modern church is that "we don't need to tell people what God is against; we just need to tell them what He can do for them." We have come a long way from the "wrong side of the tracks," haven't we? We love God, and God loves us, and that is all that matters. We are rich, increased with goods, and have need of nothing. This kingdom that is coming can't get here soon enough!

ENDNOTES

1. "The Complete Transcript of Netanyahu's Address to Congress," *The Washington Post,* March 3, 2015, http://www .washingtonpost.com/news/post-politics/wp/2015/03/03/full-text -netanyahus-address-to-congress/; March 3, 2015.

2. "Some Israelis Insulted by Obama Picture," *CBS News,* June 9, 2009; http://www.cbsnews.com/news/some-israelis -insulted-by-obama-picture.

CHAPTER 2

JUDAS THE BETRAYER

HISTORY HAS NEVER been kind to Judas. His name, after all, is synonymous with betrayal. Throughout Scripture, the name Judas Iscariot isn't mentioned without the caveat, "he who betrayed Christ." Was he hated by the other disciples? What role did he play in the itinerate ministry of Jesus? Why did Jesus choose him, and what went wrong? These are just a few of the questions about this often misunderstood disciple.

Some have suggested that Christ only chose Judas because He knew that he would betray Him. Still others believe that Jesus and Judas were working together to accomplish the plan of salvation. The Bible, however, paints a much different picture of the man Judas Iscariot.

He heralded from a relatively small village about ten miles from Hebron in the Judean province of Kerioth. From all indications, Judas was a natural-born administrator. It is altogether likely that he was looked up to as a very capable and prudent man by those around him. While we are not given many views into his life in the biblical narrative, those that are shared speak volumes. In today's culture, he would be seen as one of the highest-ranking officials in the group. Although not a part of the inner sanctum of leadership, his role was vital.

The kingdom of heaven was in motion. Jesus had begun His ministry in Galilee, home to all of the disciples except Judas. Each of them had received the same authority by Jesus. Judas had personally witnessed 37 separately recorded miracles of Jesus. He, along with the other disciples, had been given power to heal the sick, cleanse the lepers, raise the dead, and cast out devils. There was no difference placed upon Judas.

When they returned from one ministry trip, they all marveled at the power of God that had worked through them and declared, "Even the devils are subject unto us through thy name" (Luke 10:17). Jesus said to them, "Blessed are the eyes which see the things that ye see: For I tell you, that many prophets and kings have desired to see those things which ye see, and have not seen them; and to hear those things which ye hear, and have not heard them" (Luke 10:23–24).

Christ told them how blessed they were, and He reminded them in Luke 10:20 that their rejoicing should not be over the fact that demons were subject to them, but that their names were written in heaven. Judas had received the same commission as the others; he walked in the same authority and with the same Jesus as the others. For three-and-a-half years, he had walked hand-in-hand with the Master. As you read through the Gospels, there is no indication that anyone other than Christ knew what would become of Judas. The name Judas (*Jehudah* in the Greek) means to praise or celebrate, and he seemed to be the perfect team player.

In the commissioning of the seventy in the tenth chapter of Matthew there is a warning issued by Christ. Through it we can see something that is very important.

Who do I Think I am?

Jesus said to them, "Freely ye have received, freely give" (Matt. 10:8). Why would Jesus add these words? Do they give us insight into the potential we all possess to see ourselves in a greater context than we were designed to have? Did He see within them the potential to think that they were somehow like the Jewish exorcisers who pretended to cast out demons—or like the physicians who healed the sick? Both were accustomed to receiving pay.

Perhaps it seems strange that they should be told to minister freely. Because of their many misconceptions of the nature of Christ's work, not only would Judas Iscariot have been happy enough to pad his personal account in miraculous healing for pay, but others also might have seen no impropriety in receiving compensation for conferring such important benefits.

Jesus told them to freely give just as they had freely received. They had not purchased the power of miraculous healing. They had not obtained it by long, expensive study and laborious practice; it was received as a gift and must be exercised in like manner.

The framework for the ministry was laid out quite well, and they knew what was expected of them. While they were to work miracles and teach the people, the Father would take care of them and meet each of their needs. But somewhere along the way something began to change in Judas; somehow he lost focus on what it was all about and what his role was to be.

How focused am I?

One of the rare glimpses into the life of Judas is given to us in twelfth chapter of John. It is important to know that this event was only a few days before the betrayal; until this time, there is no real evidence that Judas was stealing from the ministry. But it is referred to in the context, so perhaps it had begun some time earlier. In the narrative, we find Judas watching one of the most beautiful events in all of Scripture.

Jesus is having dinner in the house of Simon the leper and fellowshipping with His dear friend Lazarus whom He had recently raised from the dead. Martha is busy in the kitchen, and Mary is anointing the feet of Jesus with oil. He can't believe what he is seeing. Kneeling there on the floor at the feet of Jesus is a woman who is wasting potentially a year's worth of wages and just pouring it out.

"Why doesn't someone stop her?" Judas asked. "The oil could be sold, and we could give the money to the poor."

> This he said, not that he cared for the poor; but because he was a thief, and had the bag, and bare what was put therein.
>
> —JOHN 12:6

In the context of this event, which occurred less than two weeks before the crucifixion, the Bible shows us three important things about Judas. We are given an insight into the real Judas. The depth of this revelation is paramount to understanding what was beginning to happen in the heart of Judas.

First, we see a pseudo-love for the poor. His words express deep concern for those who are in need. He speaks freely of his desire to take care of the less fortunate. It all sounds so good, doesn't it? He gives the impression that he cares for the poor, but his real heart is not for the poor at all. Second, we are told that he "had the bag." He had let his position as treasurer go to his head. Pride had entered in, and that pride is born out in the actions that follow. Last, he "bare what was inside of the bag." The word *bare* comes from the Greek word, *bastadzo* which means "to remove." Somewhere along the way, Judas had forgotten why he was carrying the bag. He forgot that the money was not his; it belonged to the kingdom. When he reached into that bag to steal kingdom money, he opened a door that would lead to his demise. His love for money became the root of evil that would someday leave him hanging.

There is something else about him that is important to understand—and that insight is found in the statement that "he carried the bag." It is this single fact that I want to take a little deeper look at, for it forms the framework of the full revelation.

HE CARRIED THE BAG

What is it about that phrase that could be so important? Why was Judas even chosen to be a player in such a powerful ministry? Surely Christ knew who and what he was. Was he always a thief? Why was such a man chosen to be one of the twelve?

As keeper of the bag, we understand that Judas served as treasurer to the greatest ministry ever to exist. He was the treasurer to Jesus Christ. That fact that he was appointed to such an office of trust in the apostolic community indicates that he must have been looked up to by the others as an able and prudent man, a good administrator. And there is probably no reason to doubt that he possessed the natural gift of administration or of government. There was a need among the disciples for a man of just such talents as Judas possessed—the talent for managing business affairs.

Furthermore, it seems this natural-born administrator had forgotten why it was that he was serving in this

15

capacity, and his attention went from the kingdom of God to his own kingdom. While all of these things are important and deserving of our attention, the simple fact is that Judas as treasurer embodied the role of government in the ministry team of Jesus Christ.

The mother of James and John tried to propel them into a governmental role, but she met a fairly stiff rebuke. Likewise, the religious world has tried to place Simon Peter into a governmental role in this kingdom of God, but that also was not his intended position. This leaves Judas, not one of the three "most important" disciples, but a man who had been entrusted with the financial structure of the work—or who was, at the very least, the ministry treasurer. That, I believe, is the reason the other disciples did not think it strange for Judas to get up and walk out of Passover when he did. They recognized something that was evidently quite normal. From their perspective, Judas was apparently fulfilling a direct order from Jesus.

Passover is too holy a night for someone to simply get up and leave. It is the most sacred of Jewish celebrations. It commemorates the great exodus of God's chosen people and celebrates the Passover lamb—yet Judas left and no one raised an eyebrow. They must have been accustomed to him going in and out while taking care of purchases and the administration of the day-to-day operations. He carried the purse.

Some have suggested that Judas committed his treasonous act so as to push Christ into setting up His kingdom on Earth. I have heard it taught that his "intentions were pure, and we must not be hard on him." However, the Bible does not support that argument. Actually, the Bible very clearly explains what could cause this treasurer, this representative of government, to turn on the kingdom. There were no pure motives involved, quite the contrary. There was something much more sinister at work in the heart of Judas.

Within the heart of this prominent member of the ministry team of Jesus a door had been opened, a door that would allow the darkness of Satan himself to enter. The satanic influence was about to take him to the lowest ebb. What started out so well quickly became a tragedy in the making, one that would forever change the meaning of his name from "celebrated" to "betrayer."

After more than three years of following Christ, there was a change. He who had come out of nowhere, who had risen to great authority and been given a great office, was about to commit the most heinous act in history.

When you carry the purse of Christ, you are yoked to His ability, but when you choose the purse of the world, you rely upon a failing system of provision. The moment that Judas chose to become the treasurer for the eternal kingdom he walked in kingdom authority. To whom much is given, much will be required—and for this once empowered follower of Christ, the Day of Judgment will be very harsh.

Likewise, the nation of America has enjoyed divine providence as long as we walked in covenant with God and with His people Israel. Yet now we are witnessing the unraveling of the nation. We have placed our trust and put our faith in the god of this world, and as a result, we who have been given so much are so much more responsible. I fear the judgment that is coming!

Chapter 3

AMERICA AND THE SPIRIT OF ANTICHRIST

If we ever forget that we are One Nation Under God, then we will be a nation gone under.
—President Ronald Reagan

It is impossible to rightly govern the world without God and the Bible.
—George Washington

America's rise to prominence, like that of Judas Iscariot, was by God's choosing; there is nothing that anyone can attribute our success to other than that. Although many modern revisionists are trying to write God out of our history and our president insists that we are not a Christian nation, still more than 70 percent of Americans consider themselves Christian.

Representative Randy Forbes, Republican of Virginia, founder and chairman of the Congressional Prayer Caucus wrote the following op-ed for U.S. News on May 7, 2009:

> On April 6, 2009, President Obama, speaking halfway across the world in Turkey, effectively made a shocking proclamation: that the United States did not consider itself a Judeo-Christian nation....

Our nation's history provides overwhelming evidence that America was birthed upon Judeo-Christian principles. The first act of America's first Congress in 1774 was to ask a minister to open with prayer and to lead Congress in the reading of four chapters of the Bible. In 1776, in approving the Declaration of Independence, our founders acknowledged that all men "are endowed by their Creator with certain unalienable rights..." and noted that they were relying "on the protection of Divine Providence" in the founding of this country. John Quincy Adams said, "The Declaration of Independence laid the cornerstone of human government upon the first precepts of Christianity."...

Presidents Washington, Adams, Jefferson, Jackson, McKinley, Teddy Roosevelt, Wilson, Hoover, FDR, Truman, Eisenhower, Kennedy, and Reagan all referenced the importance of Judeo-Christian principles in the birth and growth of our country.... After [the] great war, Congress came together and jointly recognized that our strength was not in our weapons, our economic institutions, or the wisdom of our committees—it is in God. Congress therefore adopted "In God We Trust" as our national motto.

So, if America was birthed upon Judeo-Christian principles, at what point in time did our nation cease to be Judeo-Christian?...[T]he answer is clear...we have never ceased to be a Judeo-Christian nation....Indeed, these beliefs are so interwoven into the tapestry of freedom and liberty upon which our nation is built that to begin to unravel one is to begin to unravel the other.[1]

When our founding fathers were developing the original design for the official seal for the United States—a proposal by Benjamin Franklin depicted the Israelites crossing the Red Sea with Pharaoh in pursuit and Moses standing on the other side. The motto was to have been "Rebellion to Tyrants is Obedience to God."[2] Another seal was chosen, but the Liberty Bell does bear an inscription from the Old Testament: "And proclaim liberty throughout all the land unto all the inhabitants thereof" (Lev. 25:10).

To those who have said that America has never been a Christian nation, or that our founders were atheists, agnostics, and deists, let us consider the facts: at least 50 of the 55 framers of the U. S. Constitution were Christians. Every single American president has taken his oath on the Bible and has referenced God in his inaugural address. Every one of the 50 state constitutions calls on God for support.

The Supreme Court, in 1892, after an exhaustive ten-year study of the matter, said, "This is a religious people. This is a Christian nation."[3] Even today, the Supreme Court opens each session with the verbal declaration, "God save the United States of America." We are a Judeo-Christian nation founded on biblical principles. In a ten-year study performed by the University of Houston, researchers examined 15,000 documents from America's founders and determined that 34 percent of their quotations came from the Bible.[4]

Contrary to revisionist accounts of the Pilgrims, their purpose is clearly stated as being for the "Glory of God and advancement of the Christian Faith." The Pilgrims were missionaries.[5] Founding father and educator Noah Webster (1758–1843) had this to say: "The moral principles and precepts contained in the scriptures ought to form the basis of all our civil constitutions and laws. All the miseries and evils which men suffer from vice, crime, ambition, injustice, oppression, slavery, and war, proceed from their despising or neglecting the precepts contained in the Bible."[6]

The early Americans knew to turn to the Bible for guidance as to how to make civil law. This was the standard for law, beginning with the Mayflower Compact all the way through the constitutions of all 50 states. America was founded to glorify God and advance Christianity, and that is exactly why God has blessed us and raised us up.

We owe all that we are as a nation to our Sovereign God who has chosen us; indeed, He ordained the United States of America to play a major role in the advancement of the kingdom of God and to be a source of friendship to His chosen people, Israel. America and Israel have been intricately knit together from the founding of our nation until now.

As Judas walked with Christ Jesus, so we have walked with Israel—and Israel has walked with us. We have been blessed by that relationship in more ways than one can imagine. Recently, on a trip to Israel, I saw a shirt that stated it very well: "Don't worry, America; we have your back!"

It could truly be stated that if it weren't for the Jewish people, the United States might not exist. It was Jewish money that was used to fund the voyage of Christopher Columbus. Money that had been stolen from the Jews during the Spanish Inquisition paved the way for the founding of our nation. Indeed, the majority of our progress as a world power has happened from the time that we recognized Israel's right to exist. We walked with them in the infancy of their existence as a nation and became their staunch supporter on the world stage.

Just before the end of the British Mandate for Palestine, which was to terminate at midnight on May 14, 1948, David Ben-Gurion accepted the United Nations' plan to permanently partition the land and declared the establishment of a Jewish state in the Land of Israel to be known as the State of Israel. Neighboring Arab States were opposed to any partition of Palestine, and over the next few days, armies of Egypt, Transjordan, Iraq, and Syria entered the former Mandate territory. On the declaration of independence, a provisional government of Israel was established; and while the 1948 Arab-Israeli War was still in progress, the provisional government was promptly recognized by the United States.

The two decades following WWII and the wartime decommission are often referred to as the golden era of American capitalism. During this period, inflation, unemployment, and budget deficits remained at historical lows while economic growth averaged over 4 percent per year. I am convinced that we saw such prosperity because we blessed God's chosen people.

Eventually the United States became the most powerful nation in the world, surpassing Great Britain and France. Not only did we possess the greatest military might the world has ever known, but our currency was the standard by which the world was measured. We were feared and respected by every nation, and for the most part, we used that authority well. We carried the purse.

WOE TO THOSE WHO DIVIDE MY LAND

In 2008, America elected a new president, one who was determined to bring "hope and change." While much could be said about this change and what it has done to destroy our nation, it is the actions taken toward Israel that I wish to deal with in this book, particularly in this chapter.

Obama rose to power in a way that is unexplained. He came out of nowhere and marched onto the political landscape in such a way that many—not just here in America, but around the world—thought was supernatural. While I believe the United States was fashioned by God to become an end-time partner with Israel, I am convinced that our president is committed to another agenda.

From the onset, Mr. Barack Hussein Obama seemed different toward Israel and, more specifically, toward the prime minister. There seemed to be a rift between these men, and no one really knew why.

BIBI NETANYAHU

Benjamin "Bibi" Netanyahu is a former Israeli special forces commando, diplomat, and politician, and the current prime minister of Israel. Mr. Netanyahu was born October 21, 1949 (shortly after the blood moon), in Tel Aviv; he grew up in Jerusalem and spent his adolescent years in the United States, where his father taught Jewish history in Philadelphia.

In 1967, at the age of 18, Netanyahu returned to Israel to fulfill his military obligations in the Israel Defense Forces and volunteered for an elite commando unit. During his service, he participated in a number of daring operations including Operation Gift during the War of Attrition that freed hostages from a hijacked Sabena Airlines aircraft being held in Beirut, Lebanon. Netanyahu was wounded during this operation. He was discharged from the IDF after six years of service, having attained the rank of captain following the Yom Kippur War.

He is often described as a hard-liner by both his friends and his foes. Unequivocally devoted and committed to the nation of Israel and its right to not only exist but to thrive, he has stated, "If the Arabs put down their weapons today, there would be no more violence. If the Jews put down their weapons today, there would be no more Israel."[7] It is this knowledge of the enemy that has won him reelection to the office of prime minister on three occasions.

Not only has he demonstrated a keen understanding of Israel's enemy, but he has worked passionately to assist the United States in dealing with terrorism. He has provided intelligence that has proved invaluable not only in understanding the mindset of the enemy, but in devising methods to properly protect our nation. In many regards, he has led the way to keep the terrorist nations at bay and in check. While America has been an ardent supporter of Israeli sovereignty and has fought hard to protect this once-fragile country in the face of utter destruction, it seems the tide has turned.

Barack Obama, like many of his recent predecessors, was determined to fashion a legacy that would include a two-state solution. Israel would be divided, and there would finally be a Palestinian State with East Jerusalem as its capital. Mr. Obama would win the hearts of our enemies and would once again make America popular. If this two-state solution was going to happen, there would have to be some quick action on the president's part. He was going to have to convince the prime minister of Israel that it was in their best interest to stop building settlements on "Palestinian" territories.

There was a road map to follow, and it was time that Mr. Netanyahu got on the road. It was time for this political hard-liner to acquiesce and fall in line with the desires of the leader of the free world. These settlements must be stopped; this inflammatory rhetoric that the prime minister was using toward Iran and its enemies wasn't getting anything accomplished. It seems the president was going to accomplish his goal no matter the cost.

First, he must summarily wedge our friend Israel into a corner while forging ahead with establishing relationships and friendships with her enemies. In the president's speech at Cairo, Mr. Obama equated the Israeli occupation of Palestine to the way the slaves were treated in America—in essence saying that the Israelis were slave masters and the Palestinians were enslaved to a cruel taskmaster.

He spent the majority of that speech trying to win the hearts of the Islamic world, a world that has been and is determined to eradicate the nation of Israel. His words were, "America is not—and never will be—at war with Islam." Yet it is Islam that has been at war with the United States, and it is Islam that is at war with the nation of Israel.

The president stated, "The aspiration for a Jewish homeland is rooted in a tragic history...that culminated in an unprecedented Holocaust."[8] It was clearly his opinion that, were it not for the Holocaust, Israel would not exist. Were it not for the Holocaust, the Palestinians would enjoy their homeland and the world would be at peace. Never mind that the land of "Palestine" was a wasteland when the Jewish people came back home, and that it was not the actions of a demon-possessed German dictator that forced the world body to allow an asylum to the Jews. No, it was

God who gave this land to the Jewish people, and it was God who brought them back to it.

After more than 400 years of control by the Ottoman Empire, the British Expeditionary Forces captured and took control of Jerusalem, and by September 1918, they liberated the entire land of Palestine. The Sultan of the Ottoman Empire was forced to sign a treaty where he gave all of his land in the Middle East to the British and French. The British land included Palestine and what is now known as Jordan. Palestine was sanctioned as "Jewish lands" where Zionists were allowed to settle, and the rest of the land, Transjordan, was given to the Arab inhabitants.

Israeli sovereignty was established, not by the Balfour Declaration on November 2, 1917, but rather by God Himself. In the Book of Genesis, chapter 12, God says to Abram (Abraham), "I will make you a great nation; I will bless you and make your name great; and you shall be a blessing." Then God says, "I will bless those who bless you, and I will curse him who curses you; and in you shall all the families of the earth shall be blessed" (Gen. 12:2–3, NKJV). I am convinced that the blessing of our nation has been tied directly to the fact that we have blessed the nation of Israel.

We as a nation began a decline as our leadership decided that we should divide the land of Israel. Following the Six-Day War of 1967 and the massive victory of Israel over its Arab neighbors and its control of all of Jerusalem, followed then by the October War or Yom Kippur War of 1973, the process to divide Israel had begun.

President Jimmy Carter laid out a "framework for peace," and it is that basic framework that has served as part of our demise. In that framework and the subsequent peace plans, we set in motion a curse that has caused our nation to spiral downward.

The United States has become almost intoxicated with an insatiable desire to not only break the commandments of God, but to attack His commandments. It is as though we are seeing how many areas we can push against Him before He responds. Such evils as abortion and the anti-christ mindset that has allowed for sweeping approval of the homosexual lifestyle are two such examples. You cannot excuse the fact that we cast God out of our schools and government and that we replaced Him with the god of this world.

We embraced the enemies of God and the enemies of Israel. In 2001, when a group of Islamic men hijacked planes and flew them into the towers of the World Trade Center, the Pentagon, and a field in Pennsylvania after being brought down by passengers, American had reached its pinnacle as the most powerful nation in the world. On that dreadful day in September, we witnessed a threefold attack on our financial system, our military, and on our soil. We have rebuilt the tower that represents our financial prowess; we have rebuilt the walls of the Pentagon, but our soil is forever cursed. Flight 93 left a hole that billions of dollars cannot fill.

What was our response? We entered into a covenant with the enemy of Israel following 9/11. They forged an opening into our country with four planes, and we allowed that to become a cavernous opening into every part of our nation. We embraced Allah and rejected Jehovah. We teach Islam, but criminalize the teaching of the Bible. We cater to the whims of radical Islam and treat law-abiding Americans like terrorists.

We are now living in the closing hours of what the Bible calls "the times of the Gentiles." It is interpreted by many as the time between the crucifixion and the rapture of the church. It is that period directly preceding the return of Jesus Christ that is described in 1 Thessalonians 4:15, 1 Corinthians 15:51, John 14, and other places in Scripture. Following the return of Christ for His church, according to the words of Jesus, the focal point of the last seven years of time will be the nation of Israel. It is in these waning moments that we, the United States of America, now find ourselves.

God, in His providence, has brought us to "the kingdom" for such a time as this. Our beginning was miraculous, and our journey has been one testimony after another of God's hand of protection and grace. From the first prayer meetings and official acts of the Pilgrims until now, our nation has had a deep reliance upon Almighty God. We were patterned after ancient Israel in so many ways as they crossed the sea to discover their promised land; our forefathers understood that God had also brought us to our promised land. It was by official action of our founding fathers and those who would follow that this great nation became a nation under God. Our laws are based upon His commandments; our government is fashioned after His pattern. The liberties we uphold are those that are instituted in the pages of the Holy Bible.

We have been the most ardent supporter of Israel throughout our existence. There have been seasons where we have not always been faithful, but for the most part our support has not weakened. That is until now. We have come to a crossroads in this nation. We are the world's sole superpower; we speak and nations tremble. We hold the purse of the world; our dollar is the mark all other

29

currency is measured against. Unfortunately, power in the hands of man often leads to blindness in the eyes.

We have forgotten where we came from and why God has blessed us as He has. Our present leadership has forsaken the Christianity of our heritage. We, like Israel, have forsaken the fountain of Living Water and have made unto ourselves cisterns; we are trying to lean on the arm of flesh. America must return to her roots, we must return to the God of Israel; we must repent before Him. It's not too late, but we are dangerously close to the point where our president will make the move that sets us on a crash course with God.

ON THE WRONG SIDE OF GOD

Over the past few years and with much more intensity, the United States has developed a foreign policy that is on a path of destruction. We have chosen to align ourselves with the enemies of Israel, the Iranians, and even went so far as to interfere with the elections in Israel. Our president has taken the gloves off with regards to his dealings with the prime minister of Israel. He has let his pride get in the way of his leadership. Recently Mr. Netanyahu accepted the call to speak to the United States Congress, angering Mr. Obama.[9] It is not proper protocol for a leader of a nation to come to our nation without getting the approval of the president. The real issue was not whether he should speak to our congressional leaders, but that he did not bow to the supreme authority of Barack Obama.

What is at stake? What is so important that Mr. Netanyahu would take time out of his busy schedule and come to speak to Congress? Mr. Netanyahu is aware of the need for the American people to understand the danger of

Why did we make a deal with Iran

a nuclear Iran. Iran has repeatedly stated that the destruction of Israel is their ultimate goal.

Why would he not come at this pivotal time in history? Why would he not want to speak to those who represent the 80 percent of Americans who are opposed to us making an agreement with Iran that will allow them to build nuclear weapons? But the larger question is, "Why would the president of the United States not want our strongest ally to come to Congress and speak, let alone to sit down with him as well?" Is it because he broke protocol and needs to be punished? Or is it that he will not cave to the demands of the president and divide the nation of Israel? Is it that our president is so busy trying to build his legacy that he is angered when Israel continues to build housing in the area of East Jerusalem?

Mr. Obama is working feverishly to set our nation on a collision course with God. Our rise to prominence on the world stage was not so we could become great in our own eyes; it was so that we would do one thing—be a blessing to Israel. Like Judas, who had the potential for greatness, our president seems to have placed his eyes on the purse and off of the prize.

The Prophet Obadiah warns the nations of the world to keep their hands off of Israel. He speaks to those who interfere with God's chosen people and warns them quite emphatically that the measure of judgment they receive will be directly tied to the way they treat Israel. He shoots an arrow straight into the heart of America in 2015 when he declares in verse 3 and 4, "The pride of thine heart hath deceived thee, thou that dwellest in the clefts of the rock, whose habitation is high; that saith in his heart, Who shall bring me down to the ground?' Though thou exalt thyself

Pride V understanding

Verses for; Israel Isa 62:6 56:10 Jere 6:17

as the eagle, and though thou set thy nest among the stars, thence will I bring thee down, saith the LORD" (Obad. 2–3).

What is our role? What is our responsibility? According to the Word of God, our role is to be watchmen. Isaiah 62:6 warns the watchmen to "never hold your peace, never be silent," yet Isaiah 56:10 declares, "The watchmen are . . . all dumb dogs, they cannot bark; sleeping!" In America we have become so proud, so self confident that, like those the Prophet Jeremiah warned of, we are saying, "We will not listen to the sound of the trumpet" (see Jer. 6:17).

How deeply am

ISIS is not our biggest threat; neither is Iran. Our most dangerous adversary is God. He declares, "If you bless Israel, I will bless you. If you curse Israel, I will curse you!" May God have mercy on our nation, and may God wake up the church. Let the sleeping giant arise! Blow the trumpet, men and women of God.

General

If America is going to go down, it is not going to be because I am quiet or asleep. I will not aid or abet in the collapse of our nation by doing or saying nothing. We will either wake up, repent, and turn to God, or we will continue this horrific collision course with Him.

Within three-and-a-half years, Judas had risen from a bump in the road called Kerioth to the office of treasurer to Christ. Now on a shadowy night in Jerusalem, he was about to trade a great legacy for hope and change. America is on the cusp of such a decision as well; we are moving hastily toward betrayal of God's chosen people. Unfortunately, we are looking for an opportunity to kiss our future goodbye. It would have been better to never be born than to come to such an incredible hour in history and betray the reason we exist.

You are right

32

Judas had reached a point of no return; he had set his mind to move toward those who were intent upon the destruction of this teacher from Galilee and away from Jesus. Unfortunately, it seems that our nation is headed down the same road: "As Judas betrayed Christ, so America will betray Israel!"

As we race down this very dangerous path, we are failing to read the warning signs. They are clearly posted, but it seems we are so intent upon the destination that we are missing all of God's attempts to save us from the destruction that awaits us. What our leadership thinks is the winner's cup is actually a cup of wrath, the wrath of an almighty God!

THE CUP OF THE LORD

For in the hand of the Lord there is a cup, and the wine is red; it is full of mixture; and he poureth out of the same: but the dregs thereof, all the wicked of the earth shall wring them out, and drink them.

—PSALM 75:8

a warning for those who are moving away from God

There are some 32 cups mentioned in the Word of God. Twelve of these are figurative cups; four deal with the judgment of God; another four deal with blessing and fellowship of the saints; and the others deal with the reward or punishment to those who side with the devil.

Cups

I believe and preach that God is a God of love and that He would rather save than judge, but it is His love and mercy that demands justice against sin.

mercy here
judgement in eternity

33

THE CUP OF WRATH

Upon the wicked he shall rain snares, fire and brimstone, and an horrible tempest: this shall be the portion of their cup.

—PSALM 11:6

One day while in prayer regarding the cup of the Lord's wrath, I asked, "What is it that would cause the judgment of God to be poured out? What is it that stirs the heart of God to judge?" As I asked that question, the Spirit of God prompted me with this thought: "When the innocent come under attack, God always responds." When babies are killed by the millions in the name of abortion, God will respond! When the aged are a "problem to society" and euthanasia becomes a solution, God will respond.

What is the sign of a wicked generation? Drugs? Gang Violence? Homosexuality? Perversion? The sign of a people moving toward the judgment of Almighty God is when there is an attack on those who have no recourse or ability to defend themselves. God will pour out His cup of wrath. Can we not hear the blinded mob of Sodom and Gomorrah crying out from the fiery pits of judgment, "America, repent! God is a God of judgment!"?

Although it is not an acceptable doctrine in the pulpits of America's churches, it is one that cannot be ignored. God is not willing that any should perish. He is not a mean God, but that does not mean there is no punishment for the wicked. God is love. There can be no denying that fact. However, love without justice is not love. Throughout the Scriptures we read of His wrath or cup of judgment.

" THE WRATH OF GOD "

God judgeth the righteous, and God is angry with
the wicked every day.

—PSALM 7:11

He that sitteth in the heavens shall laugh: the LORD
shall have them in derision.

—PSALM 2:4

Awake, awake, stand up, O Jerusalem, which hast
drunk at the hand of the LORD the cup of his fury;

—ISAIAH 51:17

For thus saith the LORD God of Israel unto me;
Take the wine cup of this fury…

—JEREMIAH 25:15

These and many other scriptures show us we can ill
afford to continue this move toward moral relevance and
godly ignorance. America must turn; we must repent. The
lights have gone from yellow to red, and we are running
out of time.

ENDNOTES

1.   J. Randy Forbes, "Obama Is Wrong When He Says We're
Not a Judeo-Christian Nation," *U.S. News,* May 7, 2009, http://
www.usnews.com/opinion/articles/2009/05/07/obama-is-wrong
-when-he-says-were-not-a-judeo-christian-nation.

2.   "Great Seal of the United States," *Wikipedia,* https://
en.wikipedia.org/wiki/Great_Seal_of_the_United_States.

3.   "Biblical Principles for America's Laws," *Faith Facts,* June
22, 2009, http://www.faithfacts.org/blog/is-or-was-america-a
-christian-nation.

4.   Ibid.

5.   Ibid.

6.   Steve Straub, compiler, *Quotes from Our Founding Fathers,* http://www.thefederalistpapers.org/QuotesFromOur FoundingFathersVolume1.pdf.

7.   See http://www.goodreads.com/author/quotes/171941 .Benjamin_Netanyahu.

8.   "Remarks by the President at Cairo University, 6-04 -09," June 4, 2009, https://www.whitehouse.gov/the-press-office /remarks-president-cairo-university-6-04-09.

9.   David Martosko and Francesca Chambers, "Obama tells Netanyahu the U.S. will 'Reassess' Its Relationship with Israel," *Daily Mail,* March 20, 2015, http://www.dailymail.co.uk /news/article-3004187/Obama-tells-Netanyahu-U-S-reassess -s-relationship-Israel-newly-reelected-leader-shifted-position -peaceful-two-state-solution-Palestinians.html.

CHAPTER 4

THE DISCIPLES

LOVING THE CROWD AND
REJECTING THE CROSS

THE BOOK OF Luke tells us that while Jesus is speaking about the impending betrayal, the disciples were arguing about who would be the greatest in the kingdom. Lest we are too harsh on them, it would be good to look into our own hallowed halls. The twenty-first-century church is not so much different than the first-century church. We are living in the most exciting hour in all of humanity; end-time events are happening all around us. Jesus is soon to return on the clouds of glory for His church, and we are too busy with kingdom business to notice it.

Busy
V
Expect
- ing.

I'm sure that there were those within the ministry team of Christ who wanted everything to stay the way it had been. Sure, there had been hard times; there had been some near misses but Jesus had taken care of them. So the attitude was likely this: *Let's just get through this weekend, and we will go back to Bethany until things die down.* It just didn't dawn on them how temporary the euphoric moment was. *Why does it have to end? Why does there have to be a cross, a crown of thorns, a tomb? Can't we just keep doing what we are doing? As long as we are getting our feet washed and needs met, what is the reason for this rush to the cross?*

Many in the church are asking the same questions. Some have even made the argument for a kingdom right here on earth—no rapture needed, no end-time scenario, just peace and prosperity. "We are too blessed to be stressed about the Judases in our midst. This is not the time to focus on sin and judgment. We are getting our feet washed and taking our kingdom seats." Like the disciples, the church is oblivious to what Judas (government) is doing. It is a very difficult situation that we find ourselves in. We are living in the final moments of history, in the last of the last days, and yet we are missing what is happening around us.

I'm not sure if the disciples who were gathered there in the Upper Room for Passover even allowed the words of Christ to register. They each had their own agenda. Who would be on His right side in the kingdom? Who would be the greatest? They were engaged in kingdom dialogue, but not Kingdom dialogue.

This was the night they were going to have to decide where they belonged—with the kingdom of the world or with Christ's kingdom. This little crowd of disciples is going to scatter in a few hours. The Shepherd will be crucified, and the sheep will scatter. With their eyes on their own thrones, they could not see or hear the King of kings. They could not hear Him as He described the horrors that awaited Him just beyond the walls. They heard nothing of the "scattering of the sheep" or the crucifixion that awaited Jesus.

No one wanted it to end. No one wanted to face the fact that while the kingdom was eternal, the moment was not. Are we any different? Is the church in America any different? Our pulpits ring with the message of the kingdom. We rail on and on about our kingdom place and our role. Unfortunately, we have fallen prey to the same spirit that filled the room where the disciples had gathered. We see eternity in what God says is temporary. One day it will all be gone. One day soon our earthly kingdoms will come crashing down. We are in this world, but not of this world.

Listen to the prophetic warning given by David Wilkerson in 1985:

SET THE TRUMPET TO THY MOUTH

America is going to be destroyed by fire! Sudden destruction is coming and few will escape. Unexpectedly, and in one hour, a hydrogen holocaust will engulf America—and this nation will be no more....

God is going to judge America for its violence, its crimes, its flaunting of homosexuality and sadomasochism, its corruption, its drunkenness and drug abuse, its form of godliness without power, its lukewarmness toward Christ, its rampant divorce and adultery, its lewd pornography, its child molestation, its cheating, its robbing, its dirty movies, and its occult practices.

In one hour it will all be over. It's all over! Judgment is at the door! Our days are numbered! *The church is asleep, the congregations are at ease, and the shepherds slumber. How they will scoff and laugh at this message. Theologians will reject it because they can't fit it into their doctrine. The pillow prophets of peace and prosperity will publicly denounce it.*

I no longer care. God has made my face like flint

and put steel in my backbone. I am blowing the Lord's trumpet with all my might. Let the whole world and all the church call me crazy, but I must blow the trumpet and awaken God's people. Believe it or not, America is about to be shaken and set aside by horrible judgments. Many other praying believers who have been shut in with God are hearing the very same message—"Judgment is at the door! Prepare, awaken!"[1]

We are sitting on the cusp of the coming of Christ in the clouds for His church, and we can feel the earth groaning beneath our feet. Birth pangs are getting closer and closer; signs are screaming at us; and yet much of the conversation within the confines of the modern church is about the temporary and not the eternal. If we knew, really knew, what hour we are living in, we would join in the eternal conversation. We are so caught up in the excitement of the triumphal entry of yesterday that we are missing the kingdom dialogue. On one hand we are energized, and on the other, apathetic.

APATHY—A STATE OF INDIFFERENCE, OR THE SUPPRESSION OF EMOTIONS

In a meeting a number of years ago with some leaders of our denomination, we were discussing apathy within the church, when the speaker asked, "What can we as ministers do to break this trend of apathy?" What a great question. The answer is too simple for the religious hierarchy to receive it: There is apathy in the pew because there is apathy within the pulpit!

We have the greatest message in the world; we have the power of the Holy Ghost to deliver it; and we are silent. We are witnessing with extreme rapidity the unfolding prophesies of Scripture, and we are apathetic. The same spirit that worked on the disciples in the Upper Room where they had gathered for the Last Supper is at work in the church where we are gathering during the last days. It is a spirit that has proven to be one of the most effective tools in the devil's arsenal of weapons. It is a spirit of distraction.

We are purpose driven, but spiritually bankrupt. We have sold our soul to the company store and have become servants to the temporary. Give us thrones, crowns, and crowds! It was the mindset of the disciples, and it is now the primary mantra of the church. The disciples were so caught up in their own kingdoms that they were missing the seriousness of the hour. They were missing the closing moments of time with Christ and filling their time with temporary matters. The Bible describes the mood of the room as being full of strife.

As we move closer and closer to the act of betrayal and the subsequent ramifications of that act, we must be aware of the enemy's distractions. We are witnessing the betrayal of Israel, and if we open our ears, we would hear the prophets of old sound one alarm after another—but we have ears to hear, yet hear not. God is trying to get our attention, but His word is falling on deaf ears. We only hear what we want to hear.

> Jesus kept telling them there was going to be a cross, but they only wanted to talk about the crowd.

While the eleven were fighting for the best seat in the kingdom, Judas was contemplating how he would betray Christ. Judas knew that it wasn't going to be protracted; he knew what he was about to do, and he knew it had to happen that night! Judas knew that things would need to move quickly—why were the disciples moving like molasses in winter? Why couldn't they hear? Or was it that they didn't want to hear what Jesus was saying?

Surely Jesus knew that most of what He was saying was not being listened to. He must have known how preoccupied the disciples were with temporary things. They were so focused on yesterday's crowds and tomorrow's crowns that they couldn't see the Cross in His eyes. There wasn't time for conversations about who would be the greatest; there wasn't time for trivial matters to become the topic of discussion; but that is exactly what was happening. How this must have grieved the Master. He was telling them how late it was, and they were oblivious to His words. Just another last-day conversation. Or was it?

CROWDS AND CROWNS

The Seeker-Sensitive Movement

There is nothing wrong with crowded streets and crowded rooms. In the parable of the great feast found in the 14th chapter of Luke, we are commanded to fill the house. He is not willing that any should perish, but all come to repentance—so were they out of order to focus on the crowds and crowns?

The issue was that they were missing the issue. They were missing out on everything that was going on around them. The Bible says they were disputing about who would be the greatest. Their contention was clouding their attention.

What should have been a moment of awe as Jesus washed their feet was a time of confusion and strife.

How sad it is that we, the church, are reliving this very thing in the sunset of the church age. We are blessed above all previous generations; we have more stuff than at any point in history; and yet we are bankrupt of that which really matters. Like the Laodicean church, we say we are rich; we say we are increased with goods; we say we have need of nothing. Jesus is outside wanting in, and He says we are naked, blind, and bankrupt.

Friend, Jesus doesn't see the church the way the church sees the church. Unfortunately, we have relegated Him to a back room and have turned a deaf ear to what He is saying. We have offered Him a throne, but not the Throne. The message was then as it is now; it was about me, mine, and ours. Oh, how it must have grieved Him to watch them fighting over such foolishness. Who will be the greatest? There is only one "greatest," and it isn't me, and it's not you! The greatest is Jesus! He told them what He is telling you and me: "If you want to be the greatest, make yourself the least."

We have wearied the Lord of glory with our foolish conversations of personal greatness. He is trying to get our attention; there is a cross to carry, and unless you and I are willing to die to fleshly desires and take up that cross, we are not fit for the kingdom of God.

It grieves me to see the depths that the church has sunk to in order to draw a crowd. It is heartbreaking to watch those who were called to cry out against sin as they now struggle with and are intoxicated by a seeker-sensitive mentality. The Lord is saying to His church, "Come out from among them and be ye separate!" The church has become distracted, and it is destroying us.

Where is the voice of God to this generation? Where are those who have been entrusted by God to be His voice to this generation? Listen to what God says to His distracted, seeker-sensitive church of the last days:

> Woe to them that are at ease in Zion, and trust in the mountain of Samaria, which are named chief of the nations, to whom the house of Israel came!... Ye that put far away the evil day, and cause the seat of violence to come near; that lie upon beds of ivory, and stretch themselves upon their couches, and eat the lambs out of the flock, and the calves out of the midst of the stall; that chant to the sound of the viol, and invent to themselves instruments of musick, like David; that drink wine in bowls, and anoint themselves with the chief ointments: but they are not grieved for the affliction of Joseph. Therefore now shall they go captive with the first that go captive, and the banquet of them that stretched themselves shall be removed.
>
> —AMOS 6:1–7

Woe to the church that is at ease—that trusts in their own strength and ability. Woe to those who have lost track of the time; you are hastening the judgment of the Lord. Woe to those who lie upon beds of ivory and boast about their prosperity; woe to those who are devouring the lambs that have been entrusted to them. Woe to those who have forgotten the purpose of our music and worship, to those who have made vain their talents and gifts by using them to draw attention to themselves. Woe to the church that is attempting to rationalize the use of wine, but do it to cover the contempt that they have shown for the new wine, the Holy Ghost. Woe to those who rejoice in a form of godliness or anointing, but do not grieve over the lost. Woe to those who have traded His anointing for another anointing.

The modern church has been given the greatest opportunity afforded to any group of people at any point in history, but we have, for the most part, wasted it. We ravished ourselves with things to cover our emptiness; we built personal kingdoms and spent multiplied millions of dollars to further our personal agendas. All the while the sun continues to set, and darkness is sweeping across the land. Amos warns us in verse seven that there are going to be some people who are going to miss out on the banquet because of the wickedness of their own heart.

We are battling one of the greatest weapons in Satan's arsenal; we are succumbing to one of his greatest tools: The church has become distracted, and it is destroying us. There are four things that the devil uses to distract us: cares, tares, snares, and affairs. It doesn't matter to him which one messes you up as long as he accomplishes his ultimate goal.

Too many are lost in the moment to realize the moment; wowed by the prospect of our own greatness, we are missing the final hours of the church age. Cares of this life are choking out the life of the church. We are choking on self-indulgence; the King James uses the term *surfeiting:* "And take heed to yourselves, lest at any time your hearts be overcharged with surfeiting, and drunkenness, and cares of this life, and so that day come upon you unawares" (Luke 21:34).

One day a young minister in West Virginia was being escorted through a coal mine. At the entrance to one of the dim passageways, he noticed a beautiful white flower growing out of all the black dust that invaded this flower's environment. Pointing at the flower, the preacher asked, "How can it blossom in such color and radiance in this dirty mine?" "Throw some coal dust on it and see for yourself," his guide replied. When he did, he was surprised that the fine, sooty particles slid right off the snowy white petals, leaving the plant just as clean and unstained as before. The surface of the petals were so smooth that the grit and grime had nothing to hold on to; the dirtiness that surrounded the plant could not get a grip on the flower and stain or even worse overtake and kill the flower. Our hearts in some ways are like that flower; we cannot always control our surroundings.

We live in a sinful world; we live in an era where, like that flower, we are surrounded by filth. We live in a world that is saturated with self-indulgence. Though we may be unable to change our circumstances, we must change the way we react.

The church has been infiltrated by the enemy. Jesus warned us to be aware of tares that would grow up in the garden; they would so involve themselves in the root system of the church that if one were to deal with them incorrectly, both the wheat and the tare would be pulled up. How does this work? A tare doesn't necessarily look like wheat; it just needs to grow side-by-side so as to intermingle with the roots.

The enemy knows that if he can put someone in your life who can get into your root system, he can destroy the fruit before it grows. We are doing what God warned

Israel not to do—we are allowing unholy relationships to distract us from our holy calling.

The disciples were fighting over frivolous matters while eternity hung in the balance. With their eyes no longer on the eternal, they were falling into the snares of the enemy. What were they missing? What was Jesus saying to them? The picture that is painted in Scripture of this Last Supper is vastly different from that which has been portrayed in our church passion plays. Leonardo da Vinci was much more accurate in his portrayal. In his painting, everyone is fighting among themselves for the highest praise and prize, and few, if any, are listening to the Master.

ENDNOTE

1.   David Wilkerson, "The Destruction of America," *Set the Trumpet to Thy Mouth* (Lindale, TX: World Challenge, 1985), excerpted on http://www.apocalypsesoon.org/xfile-55.html.

CHAPTER 5

WHEN SATAN ENTERED JUDAS

*When Jesus had thus said, he was troubled in spirit,
and testified, and said, Verily, verily, I say unto you,
that one of you shall betray me. Then the disciples
looked one on another, doubting of whom he spake.
Now there was leaning on Jesus' bosom one of his disciples, whom Jesus loved. Simon Peter therefore beckoned
to him, that he should ask who it should be of whom
he spake. He then lying on Jesus' breast saith unto him,
Lord, who is it? Jesus answered, He it is, to whom I
shall give a sop, when I have dipped it. And when he
had dipped the sop, he gave it to Judas Iscariot, the
son of Simon. And after the sop Satan entered into him.
Then said Jesus unto him, That thou doest, do quickly.
Now no man at the table knew for what intent he spake
this unto him. For some of them thought, because Judas
had the bag, that Jesus had said unto him, Buy those
things that we have need of against the feast; or, that
he should give something to the poor. He then having
received the sop went immediately out: and it was night.*
—JOHN 13:21–30

W OW, WHAT A description of the Last Supper!
They hear it, but they don't get it.

"For some of them thought, because Judas had the bag,
that Jesus had said unto him, Buy those things that we

have need of against the feast; or, that he should give something to the poor" (John 13:29). Can they be serious? Judas had no concern for the poor. He demonstrated that in Bethany when he rebuked the woman with the oil. How could they be so oblivious? The final statement in verse 30 is so telling: "...and it was night." Indeed it was.

Jesus and Judas knew that this thing was about to wrap up: Jesus because He was the Son of God, and Judas because he was now filled with devil. Both Luke and John tell us what caused him to turn on the Son of God and what caused the horrible betrayal: "Satan entered into him." There was no honorable notion driving him, no righteous cause. Now Judas, possessed by the devil, decided it was time to do that which Satan had tried to do multiple times throughout the life of Christ.

From the first Messianic prophecy in Scripture, the devil understood that one day the seed of a woman would be his undoing. I am convinced that it was he who worked in Herod when he determined to kill all male children under two. Not only was Herod afraid of a new king coming to rule the land, but Satan knew there was a new king coming and His kingdom must be stopped. He showed up in the wilderness and later tried to kill Jesus while He was sleeping in a ship, and many times thereafter—all this in an attempt to circumvent His atoning death on the cross.

> But, behold, the hand of him that betrayeth me is with me on the table. And truly the Son of man goeth, as it was determined: but woe unto that man by whom he is betrayed!
>
> —LUKE 22:21–22

It was night, and Judas now found himself between the Rock and a very hard place. Sure, he had been slipping some funds out of the accounts and had even toyed with the idea of the betrayal, but now, here in front of everyone, he was called out. Jesus has just singled him out as the betrayer. It was odd. I mean, he knew it already, but it seemed like it was all just a game until now. Judas had known for some time now what needed to happen; he knew that things couldn't keep going like they were.

At some point, others would find out about the funds that had been missing, but what Jesus had just said was much bigger than some missing funds. Jesus had straight up declared, "The hand of the betrayer is with Me on the table." With one hand on the Lord's table and the other hand being pulled by the enemy, Judas knew it was now time for action.

There comes a point when you are forced to decide whose side you are on. Live or die, sink or swim, you have to make a decision, and that is exactly what Judas did. Though Jesus had made it extremely clear, amazingly no one understood it...but Judas. He understood all too well. In one sentence we are told that he drank communion with Christ and then became possessed of the devil. At that moment he accepted his decision and chose to live with whatever consequences might arise from it.

With the cup of the Lord mere inches from his mouth and the taste of juice still on his tongue, he turned and rushed from the Lord's table. There was no turning back, no looking back, and things could never be the same. He had chosen betrayal, and at that very moment he stepped from light to darkness. It was night. How black the night was. If the moon were full and the night sky was ruled by its light, if the light from more than 300 billion stars shone as bright as noon day, it would still be night. The street was likely devoid of people, but it was oh so full of the prince of darkness and his cohorts.

Some time ago, I had the privilege of celebrating Shabbat dinner in a beautiful Jewish home in Jerusalem. It was an incredible evening. There were about 20 of us in the group that had been invited to take part in this Shabbat meal, and what a meal it was. It was very festive and yet very spiritual. As the evening wrapped up, it came time to make our way back to the King David Hotel. Because it was Sabbath, we knew that we would not be picked up by bus and taken back to the hotel. We knew that we would be walking back.

It was an amazing night. The skies were clear, but it was just foggy enough to make the street lights give an almost eerie hue. The streets were relatively quiet as we left the house save for a few others who were evidently making their way home from gatherings like ours. Though the scene was vastly different from what it would have been on the night of the betrayal, I am still gripped by the memories of walking that late night up the quiet streets of Jerusalem. Passing by the walls of the old city and walking up the streets, I imagined what it must have been like when Judas left Jesus and the others to pursue his own agenda.

Having departed from Christ, it is obvious that Judas made his way quickly to the Palace of the High Priests. It was possibly an informal meeting where the topic of discussion was the arrest of Jesus. It seems odd and almost inspired of the enemy that this meeting was taking place at the same time that Satan entered Judas. He is no doubt led by the devil to this place where the deal would be done.

He held the purse of the ministry of the kingdom of God and had ample power and probably some funds built up—but would he be received? Would he be given an audience with the leaders of Rome and the religious leaders? How would he know where they were meeting, and how would they know him? Of course they would recognize him. What was he thinking?

There was something driving him that was darker than the pride and the arrogance that he had demonstrated as he rebuked Jesus just a few days earlier. Something darker indeed. The path that he had taken would prove to be blacker than the night that had swept over the old city of Jerusalem. There were no street lights to light his way; he was being led by the prince of darkness himself.

In Luke 22:53, Jesus described this as "the hour and power of darkness." While we are safely tucked away in the hallowed structures of our churches, fighting for crowns and thrones, darkness is sweeping over the land. The absence of God's Spirit within the church has created a void. Light is being overtaken by darkness. The Judas factor is at work in the church, the streets of our cities, and within our government.

Our churches, as well as our government, are moving dangerously close to the tipping point. We will either turn and repent or continue in rebellion toward God. We will return to the Lord of glory, or we will once and for all betray the one who has called us out of darkness. Our nation is hurrying toward destruction as we pursue the enemy of Israel and fight the nation of Israel. Judas moved under satanic influence to sell out Jesus. I am convinced there is a demonic influence at work in the heart of our president that is driving him.

One must ask the question, "What is driving this man to do all that he is doing, not only as it pertains to Israel, but across the board—if not a demonic influence?" When you have decision after decision that cannot be rationally explained, there has to be something else at work. Am I suggesting that the President of the United States of America is demon possessed? No, but I do believe that he is demonically influenced. How can a man walk with someone so closely and then sink to the depths that Judas sank? Would he really do what was in his heart? Could he?

When the Lord spoke to me the words on which this book is based, I thought, "Surely America could not sink to that level. Surely our president understands our divine connection. He would never betray Israel. Or would he?" We now know that there have been ongoing, high-level meetings between our government and the enemy of Israel. Unfortunately we are not trying to decide whose side we are on; we are just looking for the right time for the betrayal. The act of betrayal has been in motion for many years, but it is being culminated now while we the church are busy about our agenda. Meanwhile, Satan is arranging a meeting where the only topic of discussion is not whether we will betray Israel, but when.

WE ARE LIVING IN THE NIGHT OF THE BETRAYAL

No previous American president has had so strained a relationship with Israel as Barack Obama. As Israeli Ambassador Michael Oren said in 2010, "Israel's ties with the United States are in their worst crisis since 1975...a crisis of historic proportions." Author and scholar Dennis Prager concurred, "Most observers, right or left, pro-Israel or anti-Israel, would agree that Israeli-American relations are the worst they have been in memory." In the spring of 2011, David Parsons, spokesman for the International Christian Embassy Jerusalem, said: "There's a traditional, special relationship between America and Israel that Obama is basically throwing out the window in a sense." David Rubin, a U.S.-born Israeli author and expert on the Middle East, put it this way: "President Obama is very harmful for Israel and very dangerous for the future of Judeo-Christian civilization." The author and economist Thomas Sowell asserted that Obama's relationship with Israel had been consistent with the president's pattern of "selling out our allies to curry favor with our adversaries." Political analyst Charles Krauthammer observed that Obama had "undermined" Israel as a result of either his "genuine antipathy" toward the Jewish state or "the arrogance of a blundering amateur." In October 2012, Israeli lawmaker Danny Danon, chairman of Likud's international outreach branch, said that Obama had "not been a friend of Israel," and that the President's policies had been "catastrophic."[1]

This "selling out to curry favor with our adversaries," as stated by Thomas Sowell, is precisely what the Lord spoke to me a few weeks ago. It is this kiss of betrayal that ultimately spells out our demise. It has been systematic and began within two days of being sworn into office as the newly inaugurated president placed his first call to a foreign leader. Of all of the leaders he might have chosen to call, for some reason, he chose to call Palestinian Authority President Mahmoud Abbas. Just six days into his presidency in an interview with Al Arabiya TV Network,

Obama said that Israel must drop its preconceptions and negotiate with Hamas. Hamas is a terrorist organization whose founding charter remains committed to the permanent destruction of Israel and the mass murder of Jews.

> In July 2009, President Obama hosted American Jewish leaders at the White House and informed them that he sought to put "daylight" between America and Israel. "For eight years [i.e., during the Bush administration], there was no light between the United States and Israel, and nothing got accomplished," Obama said.[2]

The fact that there was no daylight between us and Israel has always been the plan of God. We were established by the grace of God to be a friend to Israel. Obama was wrong in his assessment; there has been daylight between the two nations from the time that we began to pressure the Jewish Nation to give up their promised land for our empty promises. "Washington Post columnist and Middle East expert Jackson Diehl wrote, 'Netanyahu is being treated [by Obama] as if he were an unsavory Third World dictator.'"[3]

In spite of the fact that Israel has agreed to more concessions than is even logical, the president continues to insist that they are not making any "bold attempts" for peace. Like Judas, we keep searching for ways to betray them. Be assured, Mr. Obama is putting plenty of daylight between himself, Mr. Netanyahu, and the nation of Israel.

THE ARAB SPRING

In early 2011, as Egyptian protesters forced their long-time president Hosni Mubarak to step down from power,

Barack Obama declared that all opposition groups in Egypt should have some representation in the country's next government. Never mind the fact that such a development would essentially ensure that the Muslim Brotherhood would be in a position to steer the new regime toward adopting Sharia law and increase its hostility toward the U.S. and Israel. That is exactly what happened.

On February 3, 2011, Israeli lawmaker Binyamin Ben-Eliezer said, "I don't think the Americans understand yet the disaster they have pushed the Middle East into. If there are elections like the Americans want, I wouldn't be surprised if the Muslim Brotherhood didn't win a majority; it would win half of the seats in parliament. It will be a new Middle East, extremist radical Islam."[4]

With the same foolishness, Mr. Obama pushed for this "Arab Spring" to continue across the whole of the Middle East, further destabilizing the region and sending many of the countries into utter chaos. That is not to say that there was good leadership in these countries or that the nations involved were being led properly. From Tunisia, Oman, Yemen, Egypt, Syria, and Morocco, the entire Middle East was on fire. I am not suggesting that all was well in Egypt or any of the other countries, but many of them were at least friendly to the West. As it turned out, Mr. Ben-Eliezer was right; the Muslim Brotherhood, along with other anti-Israeli groups, seized power throughout the region.

Can the leader of the free world, the carrier of the purse, the one who represents the government of the world be so foolish? Is it possible that he knew what the outcome would be from its onset? Surely there were people in his administration who warned him of those who would fill the void. Is it possible that his encouragement of this Arab

Spring was a calculated move? If so, why? Why would you want to see groups rise to power who are evil and who have made no secret of their evil desires?

Was this a calculated move to isolate Israel? Was it an attempt to strengthen Islam and weaken Israel? Was he bargaining with the enemy? How far would he go? Was Barack Obama looking for an opportunity whereby he might betray Israel? Just as Judas had sought for "the proper moment to betray Christ," it seems that the president is doing the same. When will he pull the preverbal trigger? How dark does it need to get before he makes his move?

As Judas Betrayed Christ, so America Will Betray Israel

The shoe had dropped and the decision had been made. We all knew it, but honestly no one wanted to think about it, let alone admit it. The Word of God has not been veiled, but none of us dare think about the implications of its warning: "There was coming a day when every nation will turn against Israel."

The nations of the world are turning against Israel. But that's in accordance with ancient biblical prophecy, according to New York Times bestselling author Joel Richardson, who writes, "Satan is using men like puppets to effect his purposes, to thwart the plans of God. And so it's not just in the radical Islamic community; it's throughout Europe. The nations are turning against Israel. They said it would never happen again. The Bible said it would happen again before the return of Jesus."[5]

That may be the case for other nations, but not America. We will never betray them; we will never turn our back on them. Countless times we have assured them, "Israel has the unshakeable support of the most powerful country in the world." "Our friendship has never been stronger..." Though these are the words expressed by President Barack Obama, they have been stated by every American president since the re-establishment of the nation of Israel. Yet here we stand, at this most strange point in history.

With one hand we are confirming and re-affirming our support for Israel, and with the other, we are meeting with those who have only one goal, the total annihilation of God's chosen people. It doesn't have to be this way. We, like Judas, have a choice to make, and it this choice that will either seal our doom or set us up to be blessed by God. How can we shake the hand of Israel and at the same time shake hands with the Iranians? How dare we call Israel our friend while empowering those who would destroy her? As Judas sought to distance himself from Christ, America is apparently seeking to put more and more daylight between us and Israel.

There had never been a better friend to Judas than Jesus. He had chosen him out of many thousands and had entrusted him with the power of the kingdom finances. He had received the power to make decisions that pertained to the daily operations of the ministry. Everything that Judas was, in a real sense, was because of Jesus. Likewise, we must understand that it is not Israel that needs us, but we that need them. We owe everything that we are to the blessings that have come about because we have blessed God's chosen people Israel.

We have marched like Judas into the halls of a world religious antichrist system and have now come to the critical moment where we are in the process of selling Israel just as Judas sold Christ. Under the leadership of President Barack Hussein Obama, we have witnessed an unprecedented rift between America and what is arguably one of our greatest allies, the nation of Israel.

FROM THE COMMUNION TO BETRAYAL

When you consider the miles they had traveled in the past three-and-a-half years, the journey that is now before them isn't very far. There aren't many steps between the place of Passover and that of betrayal. Looking back over the relatively short period of the ministry of Jesus, it's hard to imagine that someone who had been so deeply involved could turn so quickly. No one else knew; how could they? It seems they were oblivious to the events that had unfolded that evening. What a deep chasm could be felt in the heart of Jesus. This wasn't just anyone; they had walked together, laughed together, eaten together and now everything was different.

If you would have told me that we would be where we are, seeing the things that we are seeing, I would never have believed it. There was just no way that we could have gone from the role of ardent supporter of Israel to sitting down with the Iranians to help them find a way to arrive at the point of nuclear capabilities. We are meeting with the Sanhedrin; they are going to crucify our best friend. Do we actually think that there won't be some divine repercussions? *It's going to happen, but woe to him by whom it comes…*

I heard a man say, regarding his vote in the 2008 elections, "If Barack Obama is the antichrist, then I'm voting for him so we can get this thing over with." I have heard many believers make this statement over the past few years, "If it has been prophesied, there is nothing anyone can do to stop it." Listen to the words of Christ as He dealt with this mindset just before the betrayal: "The Son of man goeth," meaning the events of this night have been foretold, and it must happen; but *"woe to that man by whom he is betrayed"* (see Mark 14:21).

We know that the death of Christ was the focal point of the Old Testament and was, after all, the first prophecy of Scripture. God the Father had said that the seed of the woman would be bruised by Satan. There are over 400 prophecies in the Old Testament which point to the coming Messiah and to His life and death. Jesus Christ perfectly fulfilled every single one of them. The odds of someone doing that who was not the Messiah are too great to even figure. This was His reason for living! He came to die for humankind; He came to be God's perfect sacrifice, but woe to him by whom it came. Listen to the sternness of these words, "Woe to him by whom it comes." Jesus was not denying that it was coming, and He even knew who it was who would betray Him. He knew every aspect of His betrayal, and although it was bound to happen, it was, in the words of Christ, better for that man to have never been born.

The events that are now unfolding before us as it pertains to America's relationship with Israel and the cataclysmic curse that will come to our shores when it happens are weighty to say the least. Please understand the serious implications of empowering the enemy of Israel. Israel is the apple of God's eye, His chosen people, His beloved, His elect. You get the idea, right? What we do to Israel we are doing to God. He takes His chosen people very seriously, and He has issued, in no uncertain terms, tremendous warnings to those who would do them harm. America can't have it both ways; we cannot expect this God that we are rejecting and betraying to continue to bless us.

Judas had to know that there would be ramifications to his actions against Christ. He wasn't going to be able to betray Him and then just turn the money back in and wish the night would go away. Unfortunately, America has somehow been convinced that we can remove God from society, expel Him from every aspect of our future and our past, and nothing will change. Things changed for Judas the moment he closed the door on his communion with Christ, and they are changing for America as well. It seems that America is somewhere between the closed door of the Upper Room and the open door where the enemy is gathered. Unfortunately, we lack the desire to turn around, or we are being led headlong into the single most devastating decision in our history.

Negotiations are under way between the powers of darkness and those within our present administration. Mr. Obama and Mr. Kerry think that they are setting the tone for the meetings. They think that they are in the driver's seat, but like Judas, they are merely puppets on a string, and they are being played. The currents are moving more quickly than they can swim, and when it is all said and done, they will understand what so many have who have swum in these waters in the past have found: there is a riptide at work. There is an undercurrent that will destroy anyone who enters into a covenant with God's enemy. The United States of America is teetering on the edge of betrayal, and the moment we commit the act, we will invite the judgment of God in unprecedented measure.

Our enemies have predicted our demise, and we know that Satan would love nothing more than to see this last bastion of freedom sifted and scattered. My prayers and the prayers of the church are that God would turn the tide and somehow spare this great nation. I believe that as long as there is salt and light God can turn this country around. However, it's late, and night is closing in. Will the church arise from its slumber just in time to divert the coming storm, or will we sleep through the betrayal?

During the great battle between the armies of the north and Israel as described in Ezekiel 38–39, we find that no one stands with Israel. In that battle God declares, "I will get the glory and not man." I am convinced that we are soon to witness this final act of betrayal and as Scripture declares, "No one will stand with Israel." The name of Judas became a cursed name in just a few short steps. The name of America will be no better in the annals of history if we continue this journey.

ENDNOTES

1. "Obama and Israel," *Discover the Networks,* http://www .discoverthenetworks.org/viewSubCategory.asp?id=1521.

2. Ibid.

3. Ibid.

4. Ibid.

5. Christopher Collins, "Joel Richardson: 'Nations Are Turning against Israel,'" *The Examiner,* January 18, 2015, http:// www.examiner.com/article/joel-richardson-nations-are-turning -against-israel.

CHAPTER 6

IT'S ALMOST TOO LATE

The Son of man indeed goeth, as it is written of him: but woe to that man by whom the Son of man is betrayed! good were it for that man if he had never been born.
—MARK 14:21

HOW FAR IS too far? Why didn't Judas turn around? Why doesn't Mr. Obama turn around? Is pride keeping him from recognizing the error of his ways and turning back to the face of Jesus in repentance? It's not too late. Certainly he doesn't understand the significance of his actions, or he would most assuredly begin the process of repentance.

It appears that Judas was recognized as a ranking member of the twelve disciples (supported by the fact that he is given an audience with the most powerful members of the religious system of the day and also with the captains of the Roman government). He was allowed into a meeting with the government of the world system to sign a covenant for the betrayal of Christ. He sold himself out before he ever sold Christ. Satan entered him. What power there is in these words!

The details of that meeting are ominous. They were prophesied by the Hebrew psalmist and king, and fulfilled to the letter: "Yea, mine own familiar friend, in whom I trusted, which did eat of my bread, hath lifted up his heel against me" (Ps. 41:9).

Listen to Luke's description of the events that unfolded:

> The Festival of Unleavened Bread, called Passover, was near. The chief priests and the experts in Moses' Teachings were looking for some way to kill Jesus. However, they were afraid of the people. Then Satan entered Judas Iscariot, one of the twelve apostles. Judas went to the chief priests and the temple guards and discussed with them how he could betray Jesus. They were pleased and agreed to give him some money. So Judas promised to do it. He kept looking for an opportunity to betray Jesus to them when there was no crowd.
>
> —LUKE 22:1–6, GW

It was not odd for them to consult together to find a way to kill Jesus. There had previously been a similar gathering and consultation, when the report of the raising of Lazarus reached the authorities of Jerusalem. The plan had apparently been that a strict watch should be kept on Christ's movements, and that every one of them, as well as the names of His friends and the places of His secret retirement, should be communicated to the authorities, with the view to His arrest at the proper moment.

It must have been an intense relief when, in their perplexity, the traitor now presented himself before them with his proposals. Yet his reception was not such as he may have looked for. He probably expected to be hailed and treated as a most important ally. They were, indeed, "glad, and covenanted to give him money," even as he promised to dog His steps and watch for the opportunity which they sought. In truth, the offer of the betrayer changed the whole aspect of matters. What formerly they dreaded to attempt seemed now both safe and easy. They could not allow such an opportunity to slip; it was one that might never occur again. Here in their midst stood a ranking member of Jesus' ministry team, the treasurer. He was carrying the purse, and I believe the purse is what led to his downfall. It represented power and authority, and it also weighed too little for his liking.

WHAT WILL YE GIVE ME?

This is what it was all about. It wasn't about trying to force some earthly kingdom upon Christ Jesus; it wasn't a means to bring about a kingdom that he would be a major player in. It was an attempt by Judas to run the show. He tried it back in Bethany and was summarily rebuked by Christ. Now it was his time; he would fill this purse even if it had to be filled by the sale of the Nazarene. It was in literal fulfillment of prophecy that they "weighed out" to him from the very temple-treasury those thirty pieces of silver. The price of a slave? That is all they were willing to give for his services? Maybe they first offered him less—and perhaps he set the price and stuck to his bargain.

Regardless of who set the price, we should not miss the symbolic significance of it all, in that the Lord was, so to speak, paid for out of the temple money which was destined for the purchase of sacrifices, and that He, who took on Himself the form of a servant, was sold and bought at the legal price of a slave.

AS JUDAS SOLD CHRIST...

A full purse and an empty heart is a high price to pay for your own destruction. What will it take to purchase our undying devotion to the nation of Israel? What does Mr. Obama hope to get out of this deal? Is it really about his legacy, or is he being driven by the forces of hell? Why is he in such a hurry to seal the deal with the enemies of Israel? What is in it for him?

I am not sure of the answer, although I have my opinions, but I know this much for sure: the devil hates Israel; Iran and Islam hate Israel; and I am ever more convinced that Barack Hussein Obama hates them. That puts him in some pretty evil company. To sign an accord or treaty with anyone who desires to blow Israel off of the map is absolute foolishness. To make concessions with that country—concessions that will allow them to pursue nuclear capabilities—is tantamount to aiding them in their stated goal.

I believe the same thing is in the heart of Obama that was in the heart of Judas. Perhaps it was a deep seated desire for a legacy or perhaps it is the devil; either way, you don't do what he is doing for 30 pieces of silver.

Judas had just made a two-fold covenant, one with the devil and the other with those who sought Jesus. His purse was now full; not only did he possess the money that had come into the ministry of Jesus and the thirty pieces of silver given to him by the Sanhedrin, he also had the pride of knowing he was in control. Look at his words in the biblical narrative: "What will ye give me, and I will deliver him unto you?" Satan was playing him like a puppet, but he couldn't see it. Judas had struck a deal, and from that time he, according to the text, "sought opportunity to betray Him."

> Woe unto that man by whom he is betrayed!
>
> —LUKE 22:22

> Yea, mine own familiar friend, in whom I trusted, which did eat of my bread, hath lifted up his heel against me.
>
> —PSALM 41:9

There are those who are of the opinion that even though America is doing some very bad things, there is no way that God is going to judge her. There are some who consider the words of this prophetic warning to be too harsh. "Surely God will spare us, and we will weather this storm as we have weathered them in the past. The church will repent, and we will vote in new leadership who will turn the ship before we plunge off in the abyss that has swallowed other once great civilizations."

Friend, please hear my heart! That is my prayer as well. We often quote 2 Chronicles 7:14, which says, "If my people, which are called by my name, shall humble themselves, and pray, and seek my face, and turn from their wicked ways; then will I hear from heaven, and will forgive their sin, and will heal their land".

The burden is not upon God to heal America. Does God love America? Yes! Did He love Babylon? Yes! Did He love Rome? Did He love the Persians? Did He love Sodom and Gomorrah? Yes, yes, and yes! Of course He did. His love for them did not exempt them from judgment. The key to turning our nation is found in 2 Chronicles 7:14; it is the big *if!* Is it too late? We are standing somewhere between

69

the communion and the kiss, but we are distancing ourselves from communion and moving toward betrayal.

> If the proponents of the teachings of a "Third Great
> Awakening" are correct, then surely you would be able to
> find this healed land in prophecy. I mean surely if you can
> find Egypt, Syria (Damascus and Assyria), Lebanon (Tyre),
> Jordan (Ammon, Edom, and Moab), Iraq (Babylon), and
> Greece, you would be able to find America.

IS AMERICA IN BIBLE PROPHECY?

Is the United States of America ever mentioned in the
Bible? If America is mentioned in Bible prophecy, then
those prophecies would give us important clues about our
destiny.

From the late 1800s until today, many books have
been written that "reveal" America in Bible prophecy.
Unfortunately, they are vague statements at best that have
been erroneously applied to the United States. While I have
spent countless hours perusing these books and studying
the Scriptures, I have even shared the opinions of these
authors with my congregation. The fact is that I cannot in
certainty pinpoint a scripture that identifies America.

I can, however, show you many scriptures that either
lump America with all nations of the world in the end of
days, or by those same scriptures arrive at the conclusion
that America will be destroyed before the last days.

The Bible says that all nations go against Israel at the
battle of Armageddon. We know that God will judge all
nations because all nations have gone against Israel.

> I will also gather all nations, and will bring them
> down into the valley of Jehoshaphat, and will plead

with them there for my people and for my heritage Israel, whom they have scattered among the nations, and parted my land.

—JOEL 3:2

For I will gather all nations against Jerusalem to battle; and the city shall be taken, and the houses rifled, and the women ravished; and half of the city shall go forth into captivity, and the residue of the people shall not be cut off from the city.

—ZECHARIAH 14:2

Then shall they deliver you up to be afflicted, and shall kill you: and ye shall be hated of all nations for my name's sake.

—MATTHEW 24:9

There are some who teach that "every nation" doesn't mean every nation on the earth. Typically, they will argue that the word *all* used in Scripture relates only to those nations that the writer was aware of at the time. For instance, when Luke tells us that *all of the world* went to be taxed at the time of Jesus' birth, it certainly didn't mean all of the world. While I would agree that in some instances one could not apply "all of the world" literally, I don't think that you can use that argument to preclude that "every nation" means just that—every nation.

Scripture says in Romans 3:23, "For all have sinned, and come short of the glory of God." Does that passage mean that every person is born a sinner and needs Jesus Christ to redeem them from sinfulness? Is there any person who is not born a sinner? We know the only person who was not born a sinner was Jesus Christ, who died that all could have eternal life. So when the Bible states, "all nations," that is exactly what it means—all nations.

So if the Bible states that all nations will turn against Israel, then the only other option available is that the United States is not a nation at the end time. We certainly hate to think of this option, but this is the only other available option. Think of all the things the United States has done to kick God out of our society. Is it any wonder that God will destroy the United States as a nation?

As I stated earlier and emphatically, the United States was established on Christian principles; most of our early laws being written based on what the Bible said. Most of our founding fathers were God-fearing people, who earnestly desired a place to worship and serve God Almighty. Therefore they rebelled against England and formed the United States of America. But now, Bible reading in many public places is against the law. The Bible (God's holy Word) has been removed from schools, and the schools are facing the consequence of that removal.

The Ten Commandments, from which all of our founding principles find their inspiration, have been removed from many public places. Abortion is the law of the land, and many millions of innocent babies have been killed while still in their mother's womb. Homosexuality is also the law of the land; their wickedness protected by the twisting of laws.

I could name many more rebellious acts and many other open sins that will bring the judgment of God upon us. The question one must ask is, "Should God judge the United States, and remove His hand of blessing from us?" He removed His blessings from Israel, and He will just as surely remove His hand of blessing from this nation.

The sense of terror that I feel for our nation is palpable. It is overwhelming. I love America as much as anyone. I pray for our nation continually, and I pray for the church that even now we would return to the Lord with weeping and with repentance. I know there is a remnant of righteous believers who have not "bowed the knee to Baal." I am grateful that many men and women of God are hearing from heaven and are sounding the alarm. That is the purpose of this book and of this prophetic word.

The Lord desires repentance, He desires mercy! Although our leadership has moved like Judas from communion toward the kiss of betrayal, we aren't there yet. It's not too late *if* we will perform the *big if*. If we will humble ourselves and pray! If we will repent! I know that a great ship can be turned with a small rudder. I believe that. But dear friend, we fool ourselves if we think that God will change His Word for us. Are we any different from the countless other nations that have vanished? The only thing that has made us different is our relationship with God and His people Israel. It was righteousness that exalted our nation.

A brother in the Lord told me just the other day that God was going to turn this nation around. Everything in me wants to believe that, but if it is going to happen, it better happen fast. I recently stood at sunset on a pier at Seal Beach, California. I was hoping to take a photo of it as it descended on the horizon, but that moment passed so quickly. Just a few quick clicks of the camera, and it was gone. There on the pier I realized how quickly the light fades and darkness takes over.

HOW DARK WILL IT GET BEFORE THE
ULTIMATE BETRAYAL HAPPENS?

Darkness is, by definition, the "absence of light." We cannot blame the president for that. We cannot blame Congress for that. We cannot lay the blame on anyone but the body of Christ. Only 2.3 percent of Americans are homosexual, yet they are controlling the majority of the news, television shows, and culture in our nation. Of that 2.3 percent, most would agree that only about half of them are demonstrative or activists. Probably no more than one to two million of them are pushing the entire nation to the brink of judgment. Why? Because they won't shut up! There are still more than 70 percent of Americans who declare allegiance to the Lord Jesus Christ, but we are doing nothing to turn our nation back to God because we won't speak up!

What is the church doing to turn things around? Again, I rejoice in the knowledge of so many who are returning to the altar. I am thrilled with the knowledge that God is raising up a new generation that is not ashamed of the gospel. Nearly every day I read of another prophetic warning to our nation, another dream or vision of impending judgment. These are all wake-up alarms that serve a two-fold purpose:

One, they let us know that God is still reaching out!

Two, they tell us we are running out of time!

God is still reaching. He raised up Noah to preach to his generation before the flood. What if they would have repented? Would God have cancelled the flood? The answer of course is yes. He is not willing that people perish. Why did He send the angels to Sodom? Was it just to warn Lot? No, it was to see if there was a righteous remnant there so that He might spare it. Did God not send Jonah to Nineveh to warn them of the coming judgment, and did God not push it back? Yes! He is long-suffering. He loves each of us far more than we can imagine.

He continues to reach out through His remnant across our nation and around the world. He is speaking to many around the world and sending them to our nation to warn us of the coming judgment. He is raising up missionaries globally and sending them to America to try to turn us back.

The other aspect of His warning is to tell us that there isn't much time. Time is running out for America. May we heed the call of repentance and turn back to God while there is still time. It is hard to imagine, but in my lifetime of 52 years, we as a nation have gone from communion to betrayal. We are witnessing the implosion of our nation.

Some years ago, during what has been called the Great Flood of 1993, I was traveling to preach a revival meeting in Hamilton, Alabama, and was listening to the news. The reporter described the scene along the Mississippi River as flood waters were consuming one house after another. He interviewed a man who had been mowing his yard. He was mowing—when in a matter of hours it would all be for naught as the flood waters overtook his yard. I thought for a moment how foolish this was. How foolish to hang new draperies on the windows when the house is on fire. Is that where we are in America? Are we too late to make a difference?

CHAPTER 7

IN THE GARDEN

W E KNOW THE events of the Passover meal there in the Upper Room with Jesus and the eleven; they broke bread and communed together and then concluded the evening with a time of singing. Rising from the table at midnight, they passed through the streets and out of the town by the eastern gate of the city and, crossing the Kidron, reached a well-known place of prayer at the foot of Olivet, the garden of Gethsemane.

As they entered the garden, Christ encouraged eight of the disciples to stay there in the shadows of the garden's entrance and then invited the other three, Peter, James, and John, to follow Him deeper into the garden. His words to all were the same, "watch and pray," while He in great distress and sorrow went a little farther. The darkness of that night has never been matched.

This is where it would all take place; this was the place of betrayal. Jesus no doubt knew that at this very hour there was a meeting taking place that would climax in the greatest betrayal in history. He knew that one who had been a friend through the entirety of His earthly ministry had now entered into a covenant with the enemy.

The songs of celebration had long since faded, and it was just Jesus and His disciples there in that place of solitude.

Something was missing; indeed, someone was missing. "Mine own familiar friend..." (Ps. 41:9). These Messianic prophecies were being fulfilled to the letter, but oh how it must have stung.

It was late, and the night was eerily quiet, save the loud cries of the Master as He interceded to the Father for mankind. The garden had a foreboding feel in the early spring, as the low-lying valley now filled with thick fog. There was no doubt an encircling gloom there in the depths as drops of blood poured from His brow. "Let the cup pass" was the cry that filled the air. It was a cup of suffering that would determine the fate of all of mankind. How long He prayed we don't know, but the depth of the prayers have never been matched. Why must this night have come? Why would He be betrayed? It was indeed for this hour that He had come, but there in the garden He sought for another way.

While Jesus was seeking for another way, Judas was seeking for the time and the place where he might betray this innocent man. Scripture indicates that he wasn't altogether sure how or when this betrayal could take place. The Sanhedrins wanted a quick resolution to this "Jesus" problem. They feared a riot after having seen the celebratory entrance of Christ into Jerusalem just a week earlier. It had to be done in a manner that no one would notice. We can certainly agree that Judas, having traveled with Christ for the past three years, would know the patterns that He followed. The secret places of prayer were well-known to him, even here in the garden of Gethsemane, even in the darkness of the night he would be able to find Jesus.

We are not told how late it was, only that it was night. Darkness in a real sense had taken over, at least in the life of Judas. The devil entered him. These words speak volumes to us as we look not only at this situation, but also at that which faces mankind in these last days.

There in the garden you could sense that something had indeed changed. The night was darker, but it was more than just an absence of sunlight; something had shifted in the atmosphere. There had been an awakening of evil, an evil so black it was palpable. How do you go from an evening worship service—where you break bread with the King of glory, have your feet washed by the Son of God, and hear His sweet voice as He sings with you the psalms of David—to this depth of foreboding?

The words of Christ were clear. He had given them direction, indeed, even a warning: "Tonight, you will be offended by Me. Watch and pray." Watch for what? Pray for what? Jesus had given them ample warning of the events that would befall Him there in Jerusalem on this Passover, yet it didn't seem to register with them. How could they not understand?

There are several references in the Synoptic Gospels to Jesus predicting His own death, the first two occasions building up to the final prediction of His crucifixion. The final episode appears in the Gospel of Mark and is repeated in the Gospel of Matthew and the Gospel of Luke. The Gospel of Matthew adds a prediction, before entering Jerusalem, that He will be crucified there.

In the Gospel of Mark, Jesus predicted His death three times. In the area of Caesarea Philippi, immediately after Peter proclaimed Jesus as the Messiah, He told His followers that "the Son of Man must suffer many things and be rejected by the elders and chief priests and scribes, and be killed, and after three days rise again." When Peter objects, Jesus tells him: "Get behind me, Satan! For you are not mindful of the things of God, but the things of men" (Mark 8:31–33, NKJV).

Each time Jesus predicts His arrest and death, the disciples in some way or another manifest their incomprehension. The second warning appears in Mark 9:30–32 (and also in Matthew 17:22–23) as follows: He said to them, "The Son of Man is being betrayed into the hands of men, and they will kill Him. And after He is killed, He will rise the third day.' But they did not understand this saying, and were afraid to ask Him."

The third prediction in Matthew 20:17–19 specifically mentions crucifixion:

> Now as Jesus was going up to Jerusalem, he took the twelve disciples aside and said to them, "We are going up to Jerusalem, and the Son of Man will be betrayed to the chief priests and the teachers of the law. They will condemn him to death and will turn him over to the Gentiles to be mocked and flogged and crucified. On the third day he will be raised to life!" (NIV)

Each of these should have been clearly understood by the disciples, but the Bible says that they didn't understand until after the Resurrection. What was it that clouded their minds? Why couldn't they understand the significance of the hour and the perilous times that had come to this otherwise peaceful night in the outskirts of Jerusalem? Could Jesus have made it any more clear to them? Perhaps they heard every word that He said as He spoke of the events that were to come, but it seems as though something or someone was at work to veil their eyes.

Now, as He had many other times, Jesus had led them to a place of solitude. It was familiar to them, but tonight everything was different. The familiarity had given way to a sense of anxiety. He had told His disciples to "let not your heart be troubled" (John 14:1), but somehow trouble had found its way in.

"All of ye shall be offended because of me this night..." (Matt. 26:31). What did Jesus mean by that? The Greek word that is used for offended (*skandalidzo*) lends us powerful insight into the events of the night. Some would be guilty of each of these meanings. Some would be entrapped; others would be tripped up; and still others would give in to the enticement to sin.

But for now, it was night, and here they were, wrestling with a million thoughts of the discussion that filled the air there in the Upper Room. Thoughts of betrayal and traps soon gave way to weariness of body and fatigue. Why was it so hard to stay awake? Sure, some were much closer to the inner sanctuary of the garden, and perhaps it was darker there than the place where Jesus had asked the other disciples to stay, but was that any excuse for sleeping at a time like this?

Who should have been more awake—those close enough to hear His agonizing prayers, or those who were on the edge of the garden? In no uncertain terms, the warning had been given two times in Matthew 26:31, 34, when Jesus said, "This night." Unfortunately, the power of night had overwhelmed them, and they all fell asleep.

WATCH AND PRAY

What meanest thou, O sleeper? arise, call upon thy God, if so be that God will think upon us, that we perish not.

—JONAH 1:6

In the lower parts of that ship headed to Tarshish, we find the prophet of God, running away from his divine assignment. Running and hiding was the lot that he had chosen. Jonah had received a clear word: "Go to Nineveh and cry out unto them, Repent." God had expressed His deep desire to save that rebellious and wicked city; He just needed someone to stand in the gap for them. Jonah had heard the voice of God and knew the command of God, but instead of going and declaring the coming judgment of God, he ran.

The Bible tells us that Jonah was sound asleep. He was missing out on all of the commotion of a ship about to sink. He was sleeping through the absolute panic that had swept through the sailors on board. They were throwing everything they could get their hands on overboard in an attempt to lighten the load. They were even praying to their gods, but the storm continued to increase in severity.

The prophet was the only one who could make a difference, yet he was fast asleep. He had the only God that could make a difference, but he slept through the prayer meeting. The sailors were throwing everything they had at the storm, yet nothing worked. The captain asked the prophet a question, and it is a question to which the world still wants to know the answer: "How can you sleep at a time like this?"

How did the disciples so quickly succumb to sleep there in that garden? Was it because they had traveled so far, or because of the drama of the evening? What caused them to allow their eyes to close when they were told to watch? "Keep yourself awake" had been our Lord's admonition just a few moments earlier, to no avail.

Lest we are too hard on these men, let's take a moment and look at our own situation. The command is as strong to us as it was to the disciples. We have been told over and over to watch, to be diligent. God has warned us to not be overcome with the spirit of the age. We have ears to hear, but we cannot hear, or perhaps we are not listening.

The darkness should be no surprise to us; it should not have caught us off guard. We have been watching the sun set for some time now. I'm not sure if anyone ever taught it, but I can assure you that it was my opinion—and I think that of others—that everything was going to be good until the rapture of the church and then things would get bad. The message of the past few decades has been about a kingdom here, one of peace and love and prosperity—even now, when our nation is, at the time of writing, more than 18 trillion dollars in debt, when we have slaughtered more than 50 million babies in the death camps that we call abortion clinics, and when we are watching the unraveling of marriage on a national level. We are witnessing warning sign after warning sign, but still our eyes are heavy.

We are living in the midnight hour, and, like Lot, we have allowed the sin of this Sodomite spirit to invade our society. We have allowed 2.3 percent of our nation to declare war on the values that we have been built upon. Same-sex marriage and the homosexual agenda are being jammed down our throats, and yet our eyes are closing.

What would Noah be doing if he were alive right now? I can assure you that he would be doing what he did when the clouds began to gather in that valley so long ago. He would stand up and proclaim repentance and righteousness to this generation as he had to his. However, we are more like Lot than Noah. We are witnessing the toll of a thousand bells; the alarm is sounding: "Keep yourself awake!"

Things can't keep going as they are! The pied piper is leading us off to our own destruction, but as long as the music is playing, we just keep walking. I am trying to sound the alarm to wake up the slumbering saints, to warn the sleepy, slumbering Laodicean church. There is a shaking that is coming. There is day of calamity that is soon to befall our nation. How can we sleep at a time like this? How dare we sleep at all?

The spirit of slumber that the disciples wrestled with in the garden of Gethsemane was no different from that which had filled all of Israel, but the disciples had no excuse for their surrender to its force. Indeed, Jesus said the "spirit is willing, but the flesh is weak"—but this was no time to allow their spirits to be ruled by their flesh.

This is no time for the body of Christ to cave to the powers that be; it's no time to give in to their demands. Blow the trumpet in Zion; sound the alarm on My holy mountain! Set the trumpet to your mouth and blow it like you have never before.

It is as though there is a spirit of slumber that is at work in the church. Like Jonah, we have gone to the lower part of the boat to sleep while the world is in panic mode, throwing everything overboard. They are praying to the gods of this world, and the ship is about to sink while Jonah, the only one who had a God that could make a difference, was sound asleep. Rather than declaring the judgment of God upon Nineveh, he found a place where he could get comfortable and drifted off to sleep. The captain of the ship screamed at him, "Wake up! Pray to your God; perhaps He will save us."

Can't we hear the world? They are screaming for some men and women of God to wake up and call on our God. He can fix this mess that America now finds herself in. He wants to turn our nation, but we are taking on water faster than we can bail it out. We don't need to bail out water; we need to ask God to turn the tide! Some tell us that the world doesn't want to hear our cries of coming judgment, but I can assure you—after touring and working in the devastated city of Joplin, Missouri, following the F5 tornado that leveled mile after mile of houses and businesses— they wanted an alarm. Why do we wait until the fire has burned down the house to recognize our need for smoke alarms? How many more lives must be lost to the god of this world before we get the alarms fixed?

The Prophet Jonah was in deepest level of sleep when he was awakened by that frantic captain. This indicates that he had probably been asleep some time. Most likely, he had already passed through stage one and two where the sleep is shallower and the person is easily awakened. None were asleep but Jonah, and he was so sound asleep that he couldn't hear their desperate calls for help. What will it take to wake us up to the cries of our generation?

Our awakening is coming, and when it does, much of the church world will be like Jonah awakened from his slumber: we will be stunned. How could Jonah not hear the commotion around him? The sailors were frantic, no doubt crying out in fear as they threw everything they had at this storm to no avail. They were still going down. It was a storm like they had never seen, but Jonah couldn't see it. Why? He was sleeping when he should have been praying.

How could the disciples sleep when the kingdom was under siege? I am reminded of the parable Jesus told about a farmer who thought that as long as he kept building structures everything would be alright. Yet all was not well, and Jesus said, "Thou fool, this night thy soul shall die, then whose shall those things be?"

All is not well, my friend; there are storm clouds building, and the winds are picking up. There is a change in the atmosphere. The most dangerous tornadoes are the ones that come in the night. There are two reasons why this is the case; one, the people are asleep; and two, if you were awake, the storm would be shrouded in darkness.

I submit to you that either we are asleep or the darkness is so dark that the storm is imperceptible. How did we get here? We really have no one to blame; it's no one else's fault. We are all the children of light, and the children of the day: we are not of the night, nor of darkness. Still somehow we have let darkness overtake our light. The church gropes in the same darkness as the blind mobs of Sodom. Evil is good, and good is evil. The atmospheric shift is tangible. Everyone feels it, but we continue to slip in and out of consciousness.

"The prince of this world is come" (see John 14:30). When he came to Jesus, he had no affect on Him because Jesus lived His life wide-awake, and the devil had nothing in or on him. The spirit of slumber that is consuming the modern church cannot be blamed entirely upon the devil—that is too easy. We must take ownership for the darkness that is falling upon our land.

In the 1960s, when the enemy tried to take prayer and the Bible out of our schools, do you know what we did about it? We did nothing; we were too busy fighting over drums and guitars being brought to church to notice that society was about to expel God from our educational system. In 1973, when abortion was legalized, what was the church doing? Sleeping! While we slept, our nation legalized the wholesale slaughter of innocent babies to cover the blatant sin of the adults.

We slept through 9/11 as the nation became a bastion for Islam and Christ was pushed further and further away. We have never experienced what we are now experiencing in America. America is in a storm. Society is in a storm. The church is in a storm. The whole infrastructure of our nation is being dismantled.

At the time of this writing, we are awaiting a decision by the Supreme Court on a state's right to declare that marriage is between a man and a woman. I already know how the true Supreme Court has ruled on it, but we will find out what the court of man has to say. The signs are pointing toward a vote that will further dismantle God's laws and open the door for even stronger judgments. Everything is being redefined, restructured, and reformatted.

The Prophet Isaiah spoke a warning to a generation such as ours. He said, "Woe unto them that call evil good, and good evil; that put darkness for light, and light for darkness; that put bitter for sweet, and sweet for bitter" (Isa. 5:20). In verse 23–24, he says, "Woe unto them...which justify the wicked!"

Today we justify the wicked act of abortion; we legalize it, and the government funds it. It's main stream (fancy clinics, board-certified medical personnel, government approved.) It doesn't matter who approves it or legalizes it: God still calls it murder! It is the taking of a life that He gave.

Mark it down, my friend; there is a wake-up call coming that no one will be able to silence. There is a shaking coming to America and the church. Denominations will tremble as God begins to shake this nation to its foundation. There are going to be some stunned ministers in the coming days, stunned because of the depth of their sleep and the intensity of the alarm.

This is no two-minute warning; this is no practice drill; this is not a test of the emergency broadcast system. God is about to shake everything that can be shaken:

> For the time is come that judgment must begin at the house of God: and if it first begin at us, what shall the end be of them that obey not the gospel of God? And if the righteous scarcely be saved, where shall the ungodly and the sinner appear?
> —1 PETER 4:17–18

Hear the Word of the Lord to this generation: "For the time is come that judgment must begin…" Where is it going to start? With the household of God—that is the church! To the church of Pergamos, Jesus said, "Repent; or I else I will come unto thee quickly, and will fight against them with the sword of my mouth"; and to the church of Sardis, He said, "If therefore thou shalt not watch, I will come on thee as a thief" (Rev. 2:16; 3:3).

We need to hear the voice of some men and women of God who do not care what man can do or what they can say. I don't want to sleep through the betrayal. "Proclaim ye this among the Gentiles; Prepare war, wake up the mighty men, let all the men of war draw near; let them come up" (Joel 3:9).

We are quickly approaching the point that Babylon had arrived at. Isaiah said, "And I will make drunk her princes, and her wise men, her captains, and her rulers, and her mighty men: and they shall sleep a perpetual sleep, and not wake" (Jer. 51:57). What is the church drunk on? We are drunk on success. We are drunk on pride. To be drunk means to be tipsy, to be stimulated with a drink or an influence. What is influencing us? Are we witnessing the rise of a "spirit of slumber"? "Watchman, what of the night? Watchman, what of the night?" (Isa. 21:11) The watchmen who does nothing not only brings peril upon himself, he brings peril upon all who are under his care. If we slumber, we are endangering our nation, our family, and our churches! Set the trumpet to your mouth! Wake up! Watch and pray.

I know it's late, but we must not sleep. We are not children of the darkness; we are not of the night. We must shake ourselves and watch. We must keep ourselves awake, for the sake of a nation that is dangerously close to the edge of the cliff. I am convinced that the enemy is working overtime to soothe the church and rock it to sleep. His pillow prophets are all too eager to assist him in this effort.

> How long will you lie there, you lazy bum? When will you get up from your sleep? "Just a little sleep, just a little slumber, just a little nap." Then your poverty will come to you like a drifter, and your need will come to you like a bandit. A good-for-nothing scoundrel is a person who has a dishonest mouth. He winks his eye, makes a signal with his foot, and points with his fingers. He devises evil

all the time with a twisted mind. He spreads conflict. That is why disaster will come on him suddenly. In a moment he will be crushed beyond
recovery."

—PROVERBS 6:9–15, GW

Three times Jesus had come to His disciples, and three
times He found them sleeping. It was not only those who
were at a distance, but also those who were in a deeper
part of the garden. Again, it may have been understand-
able for those who were afar off to drift off; they were after
all closer to the outside world. But for Peter, James, and
John, it was a different story; they were close enough to
have heard the prayers and the groaning of Christ.

As I prayed over this revelation from the Lord, I
received a stiff rebuke. You see, I have been very hard on
the soft peddling preachers that fill the airwaves today. I
have openly rebuked them from my pulpit at Harvest
Christian Centre where I pastor and in churches where I
preach revivals. I have mocked their ministries and messages; that is, until God spoke to me. I now understand
that He is well able to take care of all of us. While I may
have written off some of these men who are drifting in
and out of sleep, God has not written them off. If rebuke
is needed, I can assure you that God is able to do that. If
they are asleep, God can and will wake them up.

CHAPTER 8

THE DARK NIGHT

DARKNESS AND BLINDNESS are two different things. My father suffered with an eye disease (Retinitis pigmentosa or rp) that eventually caused total blindness. One aspect of blindness that most people fail to realize is the inability of distinguishing between day and night. Likewise, it seems that the church and the United States of America as a whole have lost the ability to discern the times. It is later than any of us realize. I suppose the question should be—how dark does it have to get before we do something?

The period of time that we are living in is as dark as any America has witnessed. Some may argue that it was much darker during the time of the Civil War. Still others would say that our darkest hour was during the Great Depression of the 1920s and '30s. The reason the darkness is more intense is this: we have experienced a light that is greater than the light at any other time in history. From the early twentieth century until recent years, we have witnessed wave after wave of divine influence on our nation. That is not to say that all as been well. I am not oblivious to our nation's wicked deeds. The United States has been blessed more than any nation in history. Our land is the most fertile, our factories have produced more, and our military has reigned supreme. From sea to sea we have been blessed.

The blessings that we enjoy are tied directly to our support for the nation of Israel. This is a fact that has been documented time and time again. As we have blessed Israel, we have enjoyed blessings, when we have stood against or cursed Israel, we have experienced great calamity. Men like John P. McTernan and William Koenig have shown us the perils of cursing God's chosen people.

God pronounced a very stern warning, and it would do well for our leaders in Washington, D.C., to pay heed to it: "Woe to those who divide My land" (see Joel 3:2). We can ill afford to have God remove His powerful hand from our nation. His hand is evident throughout our history. Indeed, it was the hand of Almighty God that delivered us from the tyranny of kings. It was His hand that pulled this great nation back together following the Civil War and destroyed the blight of slavery from American soil. It was the hand of God that carried us through the dark nights of WWI and II, and through Korea and Vietnam. Only He could have brought us through the Persian Gulf wars, not we ourselves. We as a nation have been living in the brightest light that has ever shined upon our shores. We have tasted outpouring after outpouring of His Spirit, yet despite all of this, we are watching the steely hands of darkness stretch across our borders and into the church.

How dark is it? In the garden of Gethsemane only one out of twelve were praying; Christ was the only one. Eleven out of twelve were now fast asleep. When the church sleeps, the nation crumbles. It happened in the 1960s when the church allowed a few radicals to remove the Bible and prayer from our schools. It happened again in the 1970s when, because we voted in liberal politicians who appointed liberal judges, we allowed the wholesale slaughter of babies to become legally sanctioned. In the 1980s, it was the church that bought into a false sense of prosperity that has since rocked us into a state of sheer apathy. We slept in the 1990s as sin became acceptable and even winked at from the White House to the church house. We were awakened in the late '90s as we watched God put revival on the front pages of our papers and the headlines in our news, but unfortunately we squandered any sense of authority or clout that may have been ours and dozed back off. It is no wonder that we were greeted by terrorists in the first decade of this new century, or that we continue to fight them even now.

"AS JUDAS BETRAYED CHRIST...SO AMERICA WILL BETRAY ISRAEL."

We have elected a president who has catered to the desires of our enemy while cursing Israel. Even now he is seeking for an opportunity to seal the deal that will sweep our nation into its darkest night. His blatant and sincere hatred for Israel is seen in every action he takes. "As Judas betrayed Christ, Mr. Obama is determined to betray or sell Israel out to her enemies." How dark is it, Mr. President?

What I am about to write I don't write out of hatred or disrespect, please understand my heart. I am writing this because I have heard a clarion call from God; I feel a mandate that I cannot silence. I am not alone, thank God; there are many men and women who are as adamant as I am regarding this matter. God is raising up prophets who fear the coming judgment of God more than the temporary criticism of the elite.

The Word of God declares that Satan entered into Judas, and I believe that those who are leading this country are under the direction of the devil himself. One would either have to have a gross ignorance of history and the Bible, or be demonically influenced to take the actions that our president is taking. The danger is more than a matter of economics, same-sex relationships, or race baiting; more importantly, I believe, is the path he is leading us on as it pertains to God's chosen people, Israel. As a matter of opinion (and I believe verifiable fact), the free fall of our nation is in direct correlation to the way this president is treating the nation of Israel and its prime minister.

I cannot fathom the mental anguish Judas must have experienced from the moment that he was "filled with devil." To say that he was not operating rationally would be a gross understatement. There was no rationalizing his acceptance of thirty pieces of silver for the pearl of great price. You cannot make sense of anything that followed. Neither can one make sense of what is happening in Washington at this time in history.

To list all of the utterly foolish decisions of our president would fill this book to its entirety. I must, however, point out some of the most dangerous. At the top would be the way he has embraced Islam. Allah is not the God of Abraham, Isaac, and Jacob (Israel); his religion is a religion that is from hell itself. Yet Mr. Obama has again and again quoted its book, the Koran, and even honored its demon-possessed author by calling him a holy prophet. He has honored Islam and cursed Christianity. Thousands of followers of Allah were invited to fill the grounds of our capital where they bowed toward Mecca and prayed to Allah. He has consistently searched for ways to appease those who want nothing more and will settle for nothing less than our total annihilation.

THE FOOLISHNESS OF PLAYING WITH THE SERPENT

Some time ago a family in Florida made the news because of a tragic situation. They had a pet python in their house (personally, I think that is an oxymoron), and woke up one day to find the snake had killed their baby. I cannot imagine the horror that they were dealing with, but I also cannot understand the foolishness of allowing a snake to share residence with their baby girl. Likewise, I cannot understand how our president can allow the serpent of Islam to roam freely in our nation. Hear the words of these fanatics after an attack by their operatives in Texas: "We say to the defenders of the cross, the U.S., that future attacks are going to be harsher and worse. The Islamic State soldiers will inflict harm on you with the grace of God. The future is just around the corner."[1]

Additionally, our president is working tirelessly to embrace the nation of Iran and make them our new ally in the Middle East. The danger lies not only in the fact that Iran hates America, but also in that Iran is bent on the total annihilation of God's chosen people, Israel. Is it possible that, as Judas had walked with Christ throughout His earthly ministry and then in the darkness of midnight gave Him the betrayal kiss, America who has walked with Israel throughout its modern existence as a nation would now betray them?

This Judas factor must not be ignored. As I stated earlier, the Bible clearly states that Judas did what he did because of satanic influence or even possession. I believe that it is the same spirit that is driving our president to embrace an anti-Israeli stance as he partners with Israel's sworn enemy, Iran. On the one hand, Mr. Obama states that our support for Israel has never been stronger, but on the other, he meets with those who desire a new holocaust. Keep in mind, Judas dipped bread with the same hand with which he took the silver. He broke bread with Christ and then broke the heart of Christ. Likely the last things to touch the lips of Judas were the communion wine and the Savior's cheek. What a tragic fall!

America is headed toward the same fall if we continue to meet with the enemy of Israel. The more I study Mr. Obama and the decisions that he has made and continues to make, the more that I am convinced that he is being guided by a hand far more sinister than man's hand.

We are not told exactly how long Judas searched in the darkness; we don't how long it took him to find the place where Jesus had gone to pray. It is supposed by many that he likely would have gone back to where he last saw Him and then perhaps tracked Him to the garden of Gethsemane. Either way, I believe each step was an opportunity to wake up, come to his senses, and reject the darkness that was influencing him. Unfortunately, the darkness on the inside was much more than the outside.

We are witnessing the unraveling of our nation as it moves further from the light of the kingdom of God and into the abyss of a future that is absent of that light. The streets of Sodom were full after sunset; the mobs went crazy to the point of demanding the angels of God to come out so they could rape them in the streets. As we witness the setting of the sun over our nation, we are seeing this replayed. There is an evil at work in America, and as we watch the streets of this nation consumed with mobs and riots, it should serve as a wake-up call to us.

Darkness is, by definition, the absence of light. When there is an absence of light in a nation, it affects every aspect of that nation. America, like Judas, is groping in the darkness of this late hour, and we are cursing the light. Recently, in one of the riots that was taking place in the Midwest, the thought occurred to me that we should bring in every floodlight there is and light up the areas where the looting was occurring. Why? Because there are things that happen in the darkness that will never happen in the light. The further and further we run from the Light, the darker and darker grows the night; in shadows of midnight we move ever closer to the place where betrayal becomes us and destruction awaits us.

America is carrying the purse that is now full, but full of what? It sounds like silver rattling within the bag, but the noise is not wealth; it is the sound of poverty unlike any ever known. We have traded the pearl of great price for silver, but we are so very bankrupt. To betray Israel is to accept the value of wood, hay, and stubble over that of gold tried in the fire. Certainly we have not kissed them with the final kiss, and God forbid that we do, but we have the money, and we are seeking for the proper moment for the ultimate betrayal. The agreements with the enemy are done; we can hear the sound of betrayal in the heart of our government. We are inviting destruction on the shores of America that we don't understand and we cannot control.

Judas sold Christ for the value of a slave, but when all was said and done, it was Judas and not Christ who became the slave. We will become a slave to this world the moment we ink the deal with Iran, and Judas' end will become ours. We are playing with fire, and the fire will win. It is not Iran that we are dealing with; it is the prince of darkness that is leading the negotiations. What will the prince of darkness give us in exchange for the "apple of God's eye?" What can he give us? He can only give what he has, and that is more darkness.

Judas would never see the light of day again; this was a move in a darkness that would envelope him until it destroyed him. Rattle the bag, Mr. President; tell us how great the deal is that you are securing for us and for the world—but as sure as you ink this deal, you will bring a swift destruction and darkness upon us. Do you want that legacy, sir? Just one look at Judas' legacy should awaken you from your vanity. The coins he received were used to purchase his burial plot. Mr. President, what you think will bring you great power and prestige will become your destruction. What you are doing is tantamount to someone standing at the base of the mountain slope covered with loose boulders and throwing rocks toward the top. You are going to bring a mountain down on you. Please do not do this thing that is in your heart! Daniel prophesied of a Stone that would tear down the kingdoms of this world, but I pray that America is not one of those that are torn down. We are playing with fire.

The blind are leading the blind. We are being led down a path that is eerily similar to that of Germany in the 1930s. America has embraced a man who speaks with charisma, and it seems that we are buying everything that he is selling. "We have eyes to see, but cannot see." In Nazi Germany, as Adolph Hitler began his rise in power, his ascent went unabated. No one did anything to stop him, no one. Why? Were they too consumed with their own needs and the promises being made by Hitler to meet those needs? What was it that kept German citizens from seeing their rights not only eroding, but being taken from them?

> *Those who cannot remember the past are condemned to repeat it.*
>
> —GEORGE SANTAYANA

What, if anything, can be done to stop the insanity? Will we experience the same results as Germany? Has America gone too far?

"…and it was night" (John 13:30).

ENDNOTE

1. Theodore Shoebat, "ISIS Releases This Statement: 'We Will Attack Texas Again, We Will Kill Christians, and the Attack Will Be Far Worse,'" May 6, 2015, http://shoebat.com/2015/05/06/isis-releases-this-statement-we-will-attack-texas-again-we-will-kill-christians-and-the-attack-will-be-far-worse/.

CHAPTER 9

THE NIGHT JESUS WAS BETRAYED

I N THE GARDEN at this late hour, all was quiet with the exception of the deep groans of the Master as He prayed for His disciples. The ground beneath Him spattered with droplets of blood. Twice already He has gone to them; twice He has told them to watch and pray. Twice He has had to awaken them. Couldn't they see what He saw? Had they not been listening to Him when He warned them of the need to watch and pray? But there was no sound of prayer to be heard that night as Jesus agonized before the Father.

Surely they were not asleep again? The two things that He had asked of them were not for His benefit. The Father's plan was in motion. No, the watching and praying, that was for them. Why? He knew the propensity of those who had gathered there with Him was as it is with us who are gathered in the last days. Jesus warned them of the tempter's presence there in the garden. Unfortunately for them, they were indeed asleep.

The events that unfolded in the next few moments happened much faster than one can describe. We are able by Scripture to see what it must have been like there in the garden. We see Jesus there in the heart of Gethsemane agonizing for humanity. We also see those who have been entrusted with seemingly the simplest of responsibilities as they sleep. What we can't see is what is happening outside of the narrative of the Gospels.

The moment of the betrayal is near; Judas is leading the way. One can hear only the occasional rattle of the bag, the flicker of the torches, and silence—other than the marching of the soldiers and religious leaders who were accompanying him. Uncanny, unnerving silence. Maybe his plan had worked; perhaps this thing can take place without much noise. He was well acquainted with his Master's patterns and probably hoped to find Him there asleep. For this reason, he had chosen the midnight hour for his dark deed.

<u>Isn't it interesting that the enemy would choose to move in the dark of night? While the church sleeps, the enemy moves.</u> While we are sleeping, the leadership of our nation is on the move. This is it! This is the midnight hour, and the church is asleep!

Again Jesus goes to them, and again they are asleep. He warns them of the temptation that was coming, but now it's too late; they have slept through their moment. What was coming could not be stopped, and how each of them would be impacted only time can tell. But for now, the once distant flicker of torches becomes brighter and brighter.

> On they go into the night, to the place where dark meets light.

Where are the prayer warriors? Judas was able to walk into that garden unimpeded because there was no prayer covering! Where is the sound of prayer in this dark night of betrayal? Would it have stopped Judas? No, he was full of the devil. I can't help but wonder what might have been the outcome if they had just prayed. If there was nothing to gain from prayer, Jesus never would have told them to watch and pray.

In this, the closing moments before betrayal, where are the prayer warriors? Where is the church, and what are we doing to push back on the approaching storm? We have been given the charge to watch and pray. We may not be able to change the inevitable fact that all nations will turn against Israel, but we must prepare ourselves for the fallout of such decisions. More about that later, but for now let's go back to the garden.

> And there appeared an angel unto him from heaven, strengthening him. And being in an agony he prayed more earnestly: and his sweat was as it were great drops of blood falling down to the ground.
>
> —LUKE 22:43–44

The scene in this garden was much different from the Garden of Eden; in that garden, the first Adam broke covenant with the Father. In this garden, Jesus had created a new and better covenant. In Eden, Adam was driven out by an angel, while in Gethsemane, Christ was ministered to by one. The angels with flaming swords stood guard over the tree of life which stood in the midst of the garden. How the angel ministered we know not, but we must assume that it was in that strength that He arose to face what lay ahead.

Jesus could now see the first light of the torches, moving in the moonlight down the opposite slope. The blood-thirsty mob was now coming to arrest Him. The traitor was at the forefront, but Satan was leading the way. They had brought lanterns and torches with them, perhaps thinking they might find their victim hiding, or that they might have to pursue Him. But there was no pursuit; there was no hiding savior. There was no fear in the eyes of Jesus as this angry mob approached, led by Judas, the betrayer of Christ.

While the disciples had failed to prepare for the crisis which was at hand, Jesus had thoroughly equipped Himself for it. He had fought down the last remnants of temptation; the bitterness of death was past. He was able to face the coming storm with perfect peace.

In the thickening and encircling gloom all around, he must have ever seen only the torchlight glare as it fell on the pallid face of the divine sufferer.

In the glow of the torchlight, Jesus stood with blood still dripping from his brow. It was an image that would be indelibly, eternally impressed into the mind of Judas. Driven by hell itself, he leaned forward and committed the most heinous act of treason in all of history. He kissed the blood-covered cheek of Jesus.

Only hours earlier, he drank the cup of communion with Him, and now, possibly the next thing to touch his lips was the actual blood. How did it feel? The warm skin was the representation of the "bread of Heaven," and those "great drops of blood" were the first of so many to be poured out that night.

Jesus looked at him ever so deeply and asked a most poignant question: "Betrayest thou the Son of man with a kiss?" (Luke 22:48). This word *kiss* is so strangely applicable to the hour of betrayal that we are witnessing, for it means to kiss with "friendship." He pretended friendship, but blood dripped from his lips.

His directions were simple: "The one that I kiss, he is the one you are looking for" (see Matt. 26:48). I will pretend friendship, and then I will deliver Him to you. Would it be that easy? Could it be easy at all? I doubt that he could imagine how bitter the taste of betrayal would be. Was it the blood and sweat from the Master's face that was so bitter—or was it that he had just sold Jesus to those who would crucify Him?

Now time became frozen, as in slow motion, Judas watched his betrayal unfold. He watched as the garrison of men crumbled to the ground when Jesus declared, "I am He." He witnessed the miracle as Jesus healed Malchus' ear. And then, they took Him.

He could never have imagined how empty it would make him feel. Satan had used him, but there was no feeling of accomplishment as he had surmised there would be. Where was the power he had felt moments earlier, when he, the treasurer, led the crowd to the garden? How empty the bag must have felt, and yet so heavy. The weight of the betrayal could not be measured in ounces or pounds. Thirty pieces of silver had never weighed so much.

A betrayal indicates "double crossing, double dealing, a breach of friendship...to stab." It felt like all of that and more. Dare we look a little deeper at the emptiness that is born out of betrayal?

He was utterly desolate, as a storm of despair swept over his disenchanted soul and swept him before it. No one in heaven or on earth to appeal to; no one, angel or man, to stand by him. The priests, who had paid him the price of blood, would have naught of him, not even of the thirty pieces of silver, the blood-money of his Master and of his own soul—just as the modern synagogue, which approves of what has been done, but not of the deed, will have none of him! With their "See thou to it!" they sent him reeling back into his darkness. Not so could conscience be stilled. And, louder than the ring of the thirty silver pieces as they fell on the marble pavement of the temple, rang it ever in his soul, "I have betrayed innocent blood!"

—The Life and Times of Jesus the Messiah

Judas had fallen so far so fast. Only hours earlier, he had supped with the Master, fellowshipped with the twelve, and was the treasurer of Jesus' ministry. Now that bag is so very heavy; the weight of it was more than he could bear.

The lights of the torches and the cries of the mob quickly fade away as Judas watched them take Jesus. In John 17:12, Jesus called him "the son of perdition," an apt description for what he was feeling right now. *Perdition* means, "ruin, waste." Never did a man feel more loss, more ruin, or more destruction than Judas. What could he do? He could not turn back time; he could not undo his actions. He followed the crowd; he saw them take Him to the judgment hall, and he watched as his betrayal came to its ultimate conclusion. Judas had done the unspeakable; he sold Jesus to those who wanted nothing more than His utter destruction. And now it was done.

He ran back to the religious leaders, who only a little while earlier had welcomed him with open arms. They rejoiced in his coming to see them and no doubt mocked him behind his back. "What are you doing here?" they asked. He screamed, "I have betrayed innocent blood!" What did he expect from this bloodthirsty group? Their response was one of ambivalence; they were happy that Jesus was now theirs to do with as they desired, but they despised this traitor who now stood before them. What a small price they had paid to this turncoat. He was willing to receive a slave's price for his "Master." They had no sympathy for him, and they certainly were not going to give him another coin.

> Then Judas, which had betrayed him, when he saw that he was condemned, repented himself, and brought again the thirty pieces of silver to the chief priests and elders, saying, I have sinned in that I have betrayed the innocent blood. And they said, What is that to us? see thou to that. And he cast down the pieces of silver in the temple, and departed, and went and hanged himself.
>
> —MATTHEW 27:3–5

What a tragedy! To have walked with the Lord Jesus Christ, the Son of God, and now this. All is lost; it is the picture of utter devastation. Pride has brought him to the lowest of ebbs. Can you hear the sound of the money clanging on the floor? He runs; that is all he knows to do now—just run. Where can he go? Who can he run to? He is broke. His purse is empty. His office is gone. And his friends? He has none.

Full of regret, but it is too late. Judas hangs himself!

CHAPTER 10

AMERICA'S BETRAYAL

*The day is near when I, the LORD, will judge
all godless nations! As you have done to
Israel, so it will be done to you. All your evil
deeds will fall back on your own heads.*
—OBADIAH 1:15, NLT

As I WROTE earlier, America and Israel have been intricately woven together by the hand of Almighty God. Israel has had no better friend than us, and we have had no better friend than they.

Former Supreme Commander of NATO and U.S. Secretary of State, Gen. Alexander Haig, called Israel:

> The largest U.S. aircraft carrier, which does not require even one U.S. soldier, cannot be sunk, is the most cost-effective and battle-tested, located in a region which is critical to vital U.S. interests. If there would not be an Israel, the U.S. would have to deploy real aircraft carriers, along with tens of thousands of U.S. soldiers, which would cost tens of billions of dollars annually, dragging the U.S. unnecessarily into local, regional, and global conflicts.[1]

Israel has served as a buffer to stop the expansionism of radical Islam in the Middle East. Any Islamist group such as ISIS will have to deal with Israel before they attack the more distant Western countries. Looking back at recent history, we see that Israel blew up Iraq's nuclear reactor at Osirak back in 1981, as well as Syria's in Deir-ez-Zor, 2007. Iran's efforts at obtaining a bomb were also hampered by Israel's targeted assassination of Iranian nuclear scientists, and Israel is widely considered to have a hand in the Stuxnet virus. If Israel had not done all of the above, America would have had to.

> According to Maj. Gen. George J. Keegan Jr., former head of U.S. Air Force intelligence, America's military defense capability "owes more to the Israeli intelligence input than it does to any single source of intelligence," the worth of which input, he estimated, exceeds "five CIAs." He further stated that between 1974 and 1990, Israel received $18.3 billion in military grants. During the same period Israel provided the U.S. with $50 billion to $80 billion in intelligence, research and development savings, and Soviet weapons systems captured and transferred to the U.S.[2]

Israel is America's only reliable ally in the Middle East, and is the only nation there that publicly declares its support for America. Again I repeat, "America has no greater friend than Israel."

The real value, however, is not seen in weapons that have been designed by them or security systems that have been developed by them. The real value is not that they spend more than $1.8 billion dollars in American aid money here, which creates and maintains thousands of jobs. No, the real value they bring is that blessing of favor that rests upon us because we have blessed God's chosen people.

Why then has our president worked so tirelessly to distance himself and our nation from Israel? As I stated earlier, I believe that it is the same spirit driving Barack Obama that worked through Judas Iscariot. Satan has always hated Israel. Why? Because he knows how much God loves them.

In the past, Satan has had many willing partners to do his bidding as he attempted to destroy Israel. In Egypt, Pharaoh had them in his sights, but the people of God were too blessed to be cursed. He tried to destroy every male baby, but God spared Moses and raised him up to be the deliverer. When all else failed, Pharaoh attempted to push them into the Red Sea, but God opened up the sea and it became a highway of deliverance. God took them into the wilderness, and there He taught them that He was their provider and would bring them through. The wilderness should have killed them, *but God!*

In the days of Esther, it seemed as though the nation of Israel would be destroyed yet again. Satan raised up a man who was proud and wicked by the name of Haman, who hated the Jewish people and wanted to destroy them. He was able to get the king to pass a law which said that on a certain day all of the Jews in the whole kingdom would be destroyed. *But God!* Haman built the gallows, but it wasn't the Jewish people who would hang there, it was Haman. The one who wanted to destroy Israel was destroyed! Israel, God's chosen people, lived on!

The mighty Roman military succeeded in destroying Jerusalem and scattering the people of Israel, but it could never destroy God's chosen people. The Third Reich could not destroy them with their concentration camps and death marches. The cattle cars loaded with Jewish people were not fast enough to annihilate God's chosen people. Some six million Jews were murdered in approximately 15,000 death camps, but in the end it was the Third Reich that was erased.

The spirit that moved Hitler and his henchmen to attempt such atrocities is still alive today. It is embodied in men like the Iranian Supreme Leader Ayatollah Ali Khamenei who said, "This barbaric, wolflike, and infanticidal regime of Israel which spares no crime has no cure but to be annihilated."[3] According to Khamenei, Israel is a cancer, an anomaly, a country to be put in flames and condemned to disappear. They should be wiped off the map.

> In a Friday sermon on Dec. 15, 2000, Khamenei declared, "Iran's position, which was first expressed by the Imam [Khomeini]...is that the cancerous tumor called Israel must be uprooted from the region." A month later, he repeated his message. "The foundation of the Islamic regime is opposition to Israel and the perpetual subject of Iran is the elimination of Israel from the region."[4]

More recently, on Nov. 20, 2013, Khamenei told an assembly of some 50,000 Basij militiamen that Israel was ready to fall. "The Zionist regime is a regime whose pillars are extremely shaky and is doomed to collapse," he said. Israelis, he added, "should not be called humans."[5]

> Our battalions are named Imam Ali, Imam Hussein, and Bayt al-Maqdis [Jerusalem] to clarify our final

destination to the Basiji. We will not abandon our [armed] struggle until the annihilation of Israel and until we will be able to pray in al-Aqsa mosque.[6]

—MOHAMMAD REZA NAQDI
COMMANDER OF THE BASIJ MILITIA

The enemies are talking about the options [they (Israel) have] on the table. They should know that the first option on our table is the annihilation of Israel.[7]

—AYATOLLAH HOSSEIN NOURI HAMEDANI
LECTURER AT RELIGIOUS SEMINARY IN QOM

The only way to subdue the enemies is by refusing to compromise on the goals of the resistance and to remain strong; the future of criminal nations such as the Zionists will be erased from the history books.[8]

—HOJATOLESLAM MOHAMMAD HASSAN AKHTARI
HIZBULLAH OPERATIONS LIAISON,
FORMER AMBASSADOR TO SYRIA

These are the people Mr. Obama is negotiating with. This is our new partnership in the Middle East. He is repeating the actions of Judas. He is selling our friend Israel out. Iran has never made their desire for Israel's destruction a secret, so why have we been so willing to acquiesce to their demands?

According to a source in the regime's intelligence ministry, the regime is unified in this new tactic of showing a moderate face in order to deceive the West into relieving some sanctions. It is a show! Is our president ignorant of the Iranians desires, or is he complicit? I cannot believe that he is unaware of their plans; certainly they have not tried to hide their true colors. They have never in any way suggested that Israel should be able to coexist with the Palestinians and that there should be a two-state solution in the Middle East. Instead they have shouted from the highest mosques the mandate for the destruction of the "Zionist regime."

We have turned our heads as the Iranians have taken over Yemen. A country that was a "partner in the fight against terrorism" is now in the hands of Israel's devoted enemy. We have allowed the Iranian-backed Assad regime in Syria to continue to threaten Israel. We have allowed ISIS to continue to build their Caliphate in Iraq and Syria. Furthermore, we are now allowing Iran to fill the power vacuum throughout the Middle East.

The Bethlehem-based news agency Ma'an has cited a Kuwaiti newspaper report that U.S. President Barack Obama thwarted an Israeli military attack against Iran's nuclear facilities in 2014 by threatening to shoot down Israeli jets before they could reach their targets in Iran. Following Obama's threat, Prime Minister Benjamin Netanyahu was reportedly forced to abort the planned Iran attack.

Think about that for a moment: an American president threatens our most ardent ally in the Middle East for trying to do nothing more than protect themselves against a country who has emphatically declared their desire to wipe them off of the map. Who does he think he is? Is he that blind? I am amazed how bold Judas was to march into the halls of the sworn enemy of Jesus and cut a deal with them. I am equally amazed as I watch the actions of Mr. Obama as it pertains to Israel. Is he so consumed with his "legacy" that he has forgotten history's lessons?

Mr. Netanyahu is no fool. He has stated again and again; "If we allow Iran to become a nuclear nation, we will further destabilize the entire Middle East." That is happening now. On May 17, 2015, the *New York Post* reported that Saudi Arabia will join the nuclear club by buying "off the shelf" atomic weapons from Pakistan, U.S. officials told a London newspaper.

> The Saudis—who financed much of Pakistan's nuke program—are fearful of international efforts to keep its enemy Iran from acquiring a bomb, the Sunday Times of London reports. The Saudis think the deal, backed by President Obama, will actually accelerate Iran's nuke push. Saudi Arabia has talked for years about acquiring a bomb from the Pakistanis. "The House of Saud has now made the strategic decision to move forward," a former US defense official said.[9]

Right now, the Middle East is in chaos—from Saudi Arabia's war with Iran in Yemen, to the civil war in Syria that just won't end, to the chaos in Libya where multiple terrorist groups are vying for control of Libya. There are multiple calls from Islamic leaders to stop all of this infighting and unite for one goal—the destruction of Israel.

Today we are witnessing the implosion of the Middle East. It has become destabilized to the point that total chaos is the order of the day. We took out the regimes of Saddam Hussein in Iraq and vacated the premises. That vacuum was soon filled by ISIS. Now they are marching across the Middle East unabated. Iran has become the "force to be reckoned with in the Middle East" as they continue to advance their forces through Iraq and Syria. They control Yemen, while Hezbollah is their puppet in

Lebanon and Hamas in the Gaza Strip. What are we doing to stop them? *Nothing!*

When Judas betrayed Christ, he had to know that the reason the religious leaders wanted Christ was to kill Him. They spoke openly and often of their wishes to do away with Jesus. Judas knew what they would do to Jesus, and I am convinced that Mr. Obama knows what Iran desires to do to Israel.

THE SUICIDE OF A NATION

In recent days, we have witnessed a series of events that only a few years ago could never have been imagined. The United States of America has traded its friendship with Israel and God for a friendship with Iran and Allah.

A number of years ago, the news of the day was that a doctor by the name of Kevorkian was assisting terminally ill patients to commit suicide. It was a "humane way" of ending one's life. It allows a person to avoid the pain and agony associated with a terminal disease. Unfortunately, we have come to an hour when we have a man in the White House who also thinks he knows more than God. The difference is, instead of playing God as it pertains to one individual, Mr. Obama is playing God as it involves an entire nation.

On the surface, it seems impossible that we would commit suicide in this fashion, but when you consider the Iranians who are a part of this administration (Valerie Jarrett, for example), I suppose we should not be surprised. How have we arrived at this point? How long are we going to allow this to continue?

I'm not sure how long it took for those to die who were assisted by Dr. Death, but I can tell you how long it has taken for America to reach the edge of the abyss. In just a little over six years, we have gone from relatively good health to the present where we are, at best, on hospice. We are now over $18 trillion dollars in debt, and we have slaughtered nearly 60 million babies in the name of abortion on demand. We have lost our moral compass. The thing that has exacerbated the destruction of America is this: we are turning on Israel! God said that He would bless us if we bless Israel and *He would curse us* if we curse Israel.

Mr. President, you are about to bring a curse upon this nation that is far greater than you can understand. You will unleash a judgment unlike any that has ever been seen. When you reject Israel, you are rejecting God, and when you embrace Iran, you are embracing Allah. Unfortunately, our path is apparently set, and no one is calling you on your treasonous acts.

Our approaching judgment is multifaceted. We are joining in unholy alliances with Iran and abetting their goal to develop nuclear weapons that will be used by Iran and the armies of Ezekiel 38 who attempt to destroy Israel. We are also imploding as the result of our internal wickedness. As I write, we are awaiting the Supreme Court decision as to whether we should constitutionalize same-sex marriage.

It's not bad enough that we have rejected God from our society and that we are embracing the religion of Islam; it's not enough that we are entering covenants with Israel's enemies—now we are also rejecting the laws of God as they pertain to marriage. If God judged Sodom and Gomorrah, He must judge America. We are on the verge of imploding!

JUDAS HANGED HIMSELF!

America is hanging herself! We have rejected the laws of God. We are rejecting the people of God! We are, therefore, inviting the judgment of God! The moment we finalize the deal with those who seek the destruction of Israel we will have kissed our nation goodbye. Friend, we are dangerously close to that moment right now.

I once heard of an eagle that had descended from its heights because he saw a rabbit on a block of ice that had dislodged from the banks of the river. The eagle swept down and locked its talons on this easy meal. As it opened its wings to take flight back to the heights from which it had come, there was a problem. The rabbit wasn't just sitting on the ice; it had become frozen to it.

No matter how hard the eagle tried, he could not fly off with his prey. Down the river went the block of ice, the rabbit, and the majestic eagle. Closer and closer they came to the falls that would certainly bring destruction. All the eagle needed to do was let go, and he could fly back to the safety of his nest high on a bluff. But he would not let go; instead, the block of ice, the rabbit, and the eagle cascaded over the edge of the great falls and crashed to the waves below. America is that eagle. We have locked onto a direction that is going to destroy us, and our pride won't let us release it.

Just as Judas marched toward Gethsemane, we are marching toward our own destruction. We are dangerously close to that moment when there will be no way out. Every day that passes is one less day to stem the tide. We are rattling our purses and boasting of the fact that we are the superpower of the world. We speak and nations tremble; we hold the purse and can do anything we want.

Not so, my friend. Many nations before us could be called to the witness stand to testify against us. All of them would agree, "Righteousness exalts a nation, but sin is a reproach to any people!" (Prov. 14:34).

It wasn't our prowess or our greatness that has secured for us this place in history. It is not the brilliant mind of our president that has caused us to be blessed more than any nation in history. It is the hand of God that has brought us to this place in time, and it will be the hand of God alone that can restore us to that place of supremacy.

Certainly Judas did not think that he would come out of Gethsemane a hero. Surely he never imagined what the outcome would be. Recently, our president stood up to the nation of Israel and demanded that this chosen people of God give up the land that God gave them through Abraham and which they won as a result of the Seven-Day War. He demanded that they return to the pre-1967 borders, allowing Hamas access to the most crucial real estate in the Middle East and putting them within striking distance of the very heart of that blessed land.

Historically, within 24 to 48 hours following such a move, our nation suffers extensive damage from a "natural disaster." When God says, "Woe to those nations who divide My land," He is not speaking in proverbs (see Joel 3:2). He is very protective of Israel; they are the apple of His eye.

There are those who have said, "Well, pastor, these things have to happen; it's part of end-time prophecy." When I brought that argument up to God, do you know what He said? "Offense will come, but woe to those by whom it comes." God warned that Israel would be scattered and hated by the nations, but that never released the nations from the responsibility to care for His chosen people.

What I am about to say is bold, but I must say it. Many of the "natural disasters" and tragedies that our nation has endured could have been diverted. Nine out of ten of the most costly natural disasters in modern history have come within 48 hours of our president demanding that Israel divide their land. When we declare war on the nation of Israel, we are declaring war on God.

I am telling you that our nation is on a crash course with divine judgment; we cannot win without a mighty revival and an immediate about-face by our national leaders. We only need to read the history books to see what happens to those who fail to see the handwriting on the wall. Where is Nero? Where are the Pharaohs? Where are the Hitlers of the world that thought they could win this fight with Almighty God?

Please understand me; I take no joy in writing about the demise of this nation. Do you think the prophets of old enjoyed declaring the impending judgment on Israel? No, they wept bitterly, but still it came. Jesus wept over Jerusalem, but the stones were cast down one upon another just as He had declared. There is no pleasure to be found in declaring the judgment of God upon America. I love this country. I would love for nothing more than to see things line up and normalize.

I realize that in the Old Testament when someone prophesied something that didn't happen, they were taken out and stoned. I would rather be stoned to death than see this nation destroyed. I really would; I want to be wrong. Nothing would thrill my heart more than to see all of the evil just go away and peace come to the Middle East. I would love to see morality return to our nation and godly leadership arise.

As we watch the news, we are witnessing the unraveling of the very fabric of our nation. Our cities burn with the fires of racial conflicts and civil unrest. Mobs now march through our streets unhindered. In a recent protest in the city of Baltimore, Maryland, the city leaders told us how important it is for us to give space to the looters to express themselves. We are out of control. Judas went into Gethsemane thinking he was in full control and came out in total chaos. America entered into talks with Iran, thinking we were in control, and only time will tell what this nation will look like in the days ahead.

If you think it is bad now, wait until the deal is finalized with Iran. The flood gates of judgment will be opened, and darkness will fill this land before the ink dries on the contract with hell. The primary reason for our coming judgment is that we are touching the apple of God's eye.

Everything that is happening in America right now is a prelude to a nation without God. We are no different from the other nations of the world. I realize there are many nations who have cursed Israel, and I know there are illustrations that could be given of more wicked nations and more liberal governments. What people fail to realize is this: "To whom much is given, much is required." Never has any nation been given as much as we have been given and the light that we have lived by will be the same light we are judged by.

We had God; we didn't lose Him—we expelled Him. As a result, we will receive a harsher judgment. Not only is the United States at risk of a very severe judgment from God, but those who are leading the nation down this road are, in particular, on dangerous ground. Judas betrayed Christ with a kiss and tasted death; may God spare our nation the same destruction.

ENDNOTES

1.   "U.S. Aid to Israel," *Discover the Networks,* http://www.discoverthenetworks.org/viewSubCategory.asp?id=1531.

2.   Ibid.

3.   Khamenei on Twitter, July 3, 2014, https://twitter.com/khamenei_ir/status/531057306142650369.

4.   Michael Segall and Daniel Rubinstein, "20 Threats Made by Iran Against Israel in 2013," *Arutz Sheva,* January 3, 2014, http://www.israelnationalnews.com/Articles/Article.aspx/14336#.Vgi7I-xVhBc.

5.   "France: Iran's 'rabid dog' Insults of Israel Complicate Nuke Talks," *Times of Israel,* November 20, 2013, http://www.timesofisrael.com/france-says-iran-comments-on-israel-complicate-nuke-talks/?fb_comment_id=224267551079808_554396.

6.   Michael Segall and Daniel Rubinstein, "Sworn to Destruction: What Iranian Leaders Continue to Say about Israel in the Rouhani Era," January 7, 2014, http://jcpa.org/article/20-threats-iranian-leaders-made-in-2013/.

7.   Ibid.

8.   Ibid.

9.   Bill Sanderson, "Saudi Arabia to Buy Nuclear Bombs from Pakistan," *New York Post,* May 17, 2015, http://nypost.com/2015/05/17/saudi-arabia-to-buy-nuclear-bombs-from-pakistan-report/.

CHAPTER 11

THE PARALLEL GENERATION

I S THERE A biblical parallel to the disciples in the Garden and the church in the last days? If America does to Israel what Judas did to Christ and our nation comes under the judgment of God, what will happen to the church? If we are that final generation, what are we up against? There was a spirit driving Judas, and it is the very "antichrist" spirit the Apostle Paul warned us to be aware of. It is the midnight hour, and we find ourselves dealing with the same spirit that swept through the Upper Room and Gethsemane more than 2000 years ago. There was distraction and strife in the Upper Room, and there was slumber in the garden.

Jesus warned us in Luke 17 that as it was in the days of Noah so will it be in coming of the Son of man. We are indeed living in the times of Noah. There is a flood of judgment coming, and because he (the devil) knows he has but a short season, he is working feverishly to accomplish today what he has done throughout history.

> And as it was in the days of Noe, so shall it be also in the days of the Son of man. They did eat, they drank, they married wives, they were given in marriage,

until the day that Noe entered into the ark, and the flood came, and destroyed them all.

—LUKE 17:26–27

And Cain went out from the presence of the LORD, and dwelt in the land of Nod, on the east of Eden. And Cain knew his wife; and she conceived, and bare Enoch: and he builded a city, and called the name of the city, after the name of his son, Enoch. And unto Enoch was born Irad: and Irad begat Mehujael: and Mehujael begat Methusael: and Methusael begat Lamech.

—GENESIS 4:16–18

These are the children of rebellion, the children of the curse, because Cain was cursed (Gen. 4:11). These are the people of the generation that was alive on the earth at the time of the flood. Could the names given to this generation of people show us a little about the generation that will be upon the earth at the end of days?

The generation of Cain ran parallel to the generations of Seth. Seth was the side that Noah came from; this is a picture of the bride of Christ. It's what the church is called to be. As Noah was a righteous man, we are being called to righteousness. As Noah was a prepared man, we are called to prepare ourselves for the coming storms. As Noah won his family, we would do well to follow his lead. Cain, on the other hand, was the patriarch of the wicked generation that was on the earth during the "season of Noah." It is interesting that both Cain and Seth and their offspring chose names for their children that are similar but not the same.

THE PARALLEL GENERATION: GENESIS 4 VERSUS GENESIS 5

Is it possible that God could reveal the spirit of the last-days generation through the names of the parallel generation? Let's look at Genesis 4 and the names that are mentioned in the lineage of Cain, the rebellious generation:

- *Cain*: "to strike fast"

- *From Nod*: "from a place of exile"

- *Enoch*: "dedicated"

- *Irad*: "fugitive"

- *Mehujael*: "to blot out or erase the name of God"

- *Methusael*: "man of God"

- *Lamech*: "despairing"; "to be brought low"

If you take their names and lay them out as they are, you see a striking revelation. These meanings strung together indicate "one who will strike fast from a place of exile, who is a dedicated fugitive, who will attempt to blot out the name of God and the man of God, and he will be brought low." It is the Judas factor—and as certainly as it failed in the garden, it will fail now. The powers of darkness are moving in an attempt to blot out God. Hell is not content to just try to blot out the name of God; Satan still believes that he can blot out God.

THE NAME *MEHUJAEL* AND THE DAYS OF NOAH

Who were those that Noah preached to? What were they like? All of those Noah tried to reach were actually his relatives. They were all descendants of Adam. Noah, whose genealogies are given in the fifth chapter of Genesis, was described by Peter as "a preacher of righteousness" (2 Pet. 2:5).

The fourth chapter of Genesis describes a parallel generation or the generation that Noah preached to. In particular, you see the fifth from Adam mentioned in the genealogies of Cain. His name is Mehujael. The Hebrew root of this name is *Mah khah,* meaning to "blot out" and *el,* which means "God." So the name literally means "to blot out or rub out God."

The "Mehujael Spirit" was at work trying to blot out the name of God. It is that spirit which we see moving in our society today. Allow me to serve notice on the powers of hell that have tried to blot God out. God cannot be stopped, wiped out, defeated, or dethroned. What He has spoken He will bring to pass!

SOMEONE SHUT THAT BABY UP!

There is a sound that to this day sends the devil into a corner of hell where he curls up in a ball and rocks back and forth. There is a sound that causes the alarms to go off in the caverns of the deep. God told the serpent that He would be defeated through the birth of a baby. If the sound of a baby crying causes your heart to be moved; just imagine how it made the devil feel the first time the shriek of a newborn filled the sky! I wonder if that isn't why he fights to kill the babies before they get a chance to cry. Can't you hear the devil screaming: "Kill them in the womb, but don't make me hear that sound!"? Why does he hate it so? It reminds him that he couldn't blot God out in Genesis, and he can't blot him out today!

God had promised that the Messiah, the seed of the woman, was coming to destroy the works of the devil. The tempter was to be crushed by one particular seed or descendent of the woman. This is a glorious promise: the seed of the woman was to destroy the serpent. The serpent would strike the heel and bruise him, but the baby would strike the final and fatal blow. The seed of the woman would crush the serpent's head.

The curse that has been placed on Satan weighs heavy on him. In Revelation 12:12, we are told that during the tribulation he is well aware of the short time that he has to work. While I do not believe the devil is privy to all that is taking place in the plan of God, I am certain that he can hear the clock ticking. Every plan that he has contrived has backfired on him, and that will continue to be the case. From the cry of that first baby, he has known that his days are numbered.

At times, it feels as though the devil is running the show. He moved Judas to betray Christ and it worked. He moved the Roman government to destroy Jerusalem, and they did. He moved Hitler to destroy Israel, and it almost worked. The one who is in charge, however, is not the devil. The one who turns the hearts of the kings and moves men like pawns upon a chess board is God. He is still in control.

A million soldiers could not have destroyed Christ! He said in John 12:24, "Verily, verily, I say unto you, except a corn of wheat fall into the ground and die, it abideth alone: but if it die, it bringeth forth much fruit." The devil and all of his cohorts could not blot out Jesus. Historians cannot blot Him out. This generation, try as it may, cannot blot Him out. When all of the dust has settled and every bomb that man can devise has gone off, Jesus still is! He still lives! He still reigns over all of the Earth. Every knee shall bow, every tongue confess that Jesus Christ is Lord! Satan has but a short time!

What is the Judas spirit doing in the world right now? It is doing what it has always done. It is trying to blot out God. Listen as the writer of Romans describes this Mehujael generation:

> Because that, when they knew God, they glorified him not as God, neither were thankful; but became vain in their imaginations, and their foolish heart was darkened. Professing themselves to be wise, they became fools, and changed the glory of the uncorruptible God into an image made like to corruptible man, and to birds, and fourfooted beasts, and creeping things. Wherefore God also gave them up to uncleanness through the lusts of their own hearts, to dishonour their own bodies between themselves: Who changed the truth of God into a lie, and worshipped and served the creature more than the Creator, who is blessed for ever. Amen. For this cause God gave them up unto vile affections: for even their women did change the natural use into that which is against nature: And likewise also the men, leaving the natural use of the woman, burned in their lust one toward another; men with men working that which is unseemly, and receiving in themselves that recompence of their error which was meet. And even as they did not like to retain

God in their knowledge, God gave them over to a reprobate mind, to do those things which are not convenient; being filled with all unrighteousness, fornication, wickedness, covetousness, maliciousness; full of envy, murder, debate, deceit, malignity; whisperers, backbiters, haters of God, despiteful, proud, boasters, inventors of evil things, disobedient to parents, without understanding, covenant breakers, without natural affection, implacable, unmerciful: Who knowing the judgment of God, that they which commit such things are worthy of death, not only do the same, but have pleasure in them that do them.

—ROMANS 1:21–32

THE FOOL HATH SAID IN HIS HEART, *NO GOD*!

How foolish it is for the clay to the potter, "I have no need of you." How utterly foolish is this generation who declares, "God bless America," out of one side of their mouth and with the other curses Him. If the foundations of our nation continue to be destroyed, what can the righteous do?

What will happen to the church if this nation continues its free fall? If it implodes, if our economy tanks, if our government falls apart, what will happen to the church? At the end of the day, we the church must bear some of the responsibility for what is about to happen. The disciples should have been awake. They should have been praying. They should have been watching. Instead they were asleep.

Will we be left to pick up the pieces of America? Will we be scrambling around trying to make sense of the madness? When Judas makes his move and America betrays Israel, we are going to find ourselves in a state of confusion. The collapse that we are witnessing in America will not only continue, but will increase. With every new effort to blot out God, with each attempt to force Israel to accept a peace deal, a new wave comes to erode our foundation.

During the days of the second Gulf War, President George W. Bush was attacked for "trying to go it alone." The opposition party was relentless in their criticism. He was barraged by the left for not taking proper steps to "build a coalition." Whether that criticism was justified or proper is for another book and another day, but if ever there is a danger in "going it alone," it is now. We cannot survive without God! We cannot continue to exist as a nation, let alone a "superpower" without the providential power of God.

There is a vast difference between erosion and undermining. *Erosion* is defined as "the gradual destruction or diminution of something." Undermining is different; look at the synonyms associated with the word *undermine:* subvert, undercut, sabotage, threaten, weaken, compromise, diminish, reduce, impair, mar, spoil, ruin, damage, hurt, injure, cripple, sap, and shake.

If our nation is eroding, that is bad enough. We have been eroding for many years. Some erosion is natural or to be expected. With the erosion in our history, we have always seemed to recover. Each time we would be at the point of breaking, there would be a great awakening that would somehow address the weakened areas and shore up the foundations. With both of the spiritual awakenings our nation has experienced, God took what the enemy meant for our destruction and turned it for His glory. Why? Because the church prayed, repented, and turned to Him.

The difficulty that we find ourselves in as a nation today is different. It is both an erosion and an undermining of the foundation. The winds of judgment are beginning to blow, and the ramifications of those attempts to blot out God are many. Let's take a moment and look at the erosion and the undermining of America that is taking place before our eyes.

EROSION AND CLIMATE CHANGE

Because we have expelled God from our society, our educational system, and our legal system, we have began to experience a climate change. It is the mantra of the left, but what is climate change? It is by definition "a long-term change in the Earth's climate." I personally am not a believer in "global warming." It is a ruse by the left to implement rules and regulations that allow more and more control of our nation. Climate change has become their catalyst to garner more control of our freedoms. While I could get into this in more detail, I will not at this point. The change in climate that I am dealing with is much more real than that which is being fostered by the socialist agenda.

We have witnessed a change in the spiritual climate in America. Although you could track it back many years, it has intensified over the past two decades and particularly since 2001. What has caused the rapidity of change? While one could argue that the spiritual climate has been bad for many decades, you would be hard pressed to find a time when it has reached the level it is at today. It is "the perfect storm."

131

A "perfect storm" is an expression that describes an event where a rare combination of circumstances will aggravate a situation drastically. It is where everything that can go wrong does so at the same time. Since the attacks by radical Muslims in 2001, we have seen an unprecedented change in the spiritual climate of America. Why? When the enemy attacked us, we did not fall on our face and repent of our national sins as we should have. Instead of allowing this attack to wake us up to our need for God and to shore up our foundations, we did the opposite. We sang "God bless America"; our churches saw an immediate numeric growth; and we had a time of national prayer. So, was there a return to God? The answer is an emphatic *No!* We sang "God bless America," but we never repented for the sins we were committing. Our churches saw an increase in attendance but no lasting commitment to Christ. Unfortunately, our national prayer was more that our enemies would be nice to us than for God to forgive us.

You can track the major transformation in spiritual climate to the point when it became acceptable to teach Islam in the schools of America. Following the attack of Islam on America, we embraced Islam. There is not one nation on the face of the Earth that has opened the door to Islamic teachings that is a prosperous nation. There is something so dark about this religion that when a society embraces it, that society crumbles. The God of Islam is not the God of Abraham, Isaac, and Jacob. Allah is not Jehovah.

Our Judeo-Christian culture, indeed our nation as a whole, was built upon the principles of the Bible. When we allowed Imam Muzammi H. Siddiqi to call upon Allah on September 14, 2001, at our National Memorial Service, we opened the door to Satan himself. That is a door that remains open to this day. Unfortunately, we elected a president who not only left the door open, but has opened it much wider.

Muzammil H. Siddiqi, when questioned by other Muslims regarding his involvement in that memorial service, had this to say, "We must not forget that Allah's rules have to be established in all lands, and all our efforts should lead to that direction."[1] What rules was he speaking of? World domination. Islamic teachings are very clear that all of the world must worship Allah, including America.

Now, if as so many try to teach, Allah and Jehovah are one and the same, then why are they trying to change the rules of America? Not only are they attempting to undermine and destroy the biblical foundation of America, but they are attempting to blot out the God of our Hebraic roots and introduce the religion of Islam.

As our leadership continues on this path to embrace the teachings of the unholy Koran, they are inviting the demonic forces that it represents into our society. That is where you find the "atmospheric change" taking place. There is a shift in the heavens over America, and that shift is moving us from the blessings of God (Jehovah) to the curse of the god (Allah). With the climate change, comes a drying of the atmosphere, and with the winds of the enemy blowing, we are seeing tremendous erosion to our national foundation. Satan can only move in dry places.

UNDERMINING OF THE FOUNDATION

Let me remind you of the synonyms related to the term *undermine:* subvert, undercut, sabotage, threaten, weaken, compromise, diminish, reduce, impair, mar, spoil, ruin, damage, hurt, injure, cripple, sap, shake.

Scripture asks the question, "If the foundations be destroyed..." from the Hebrew word *haras* which means "to pull down or in pieces, break, destroy, beat down, break down, break through, destroy, overthrow, pluck down, pull down, ruin, throw down, utterly." Did you catch that? It is not like erosion; our foundations are under attack. We are witnessing the undermining of our national foundation. The present leadership in Washington D.C. is intentionally working to destroy our foundation. It has been eroding for decades, but now we are seeing erosion replaced by an undermining.

In Jerusalem, the Arabs have worked tirelessly to try to remove anything that could potentially connect Israel to the Temple Mount and Jerusalem, including the destruction of historical artifacts. In much the same way, our president lauds the "great influence that Islam has had in our history," but denies the real influence that God has played.

History has shown us the way to change a society is to introduce falsehood and continue to speak of it as though it were true until it is believed. Unfortunately, many in our nation are believing the lie. Christianity is under attack. Our freedoms are under attack. Our Constitution is under attack. The sanctity of marriage is under attack. Biblical morality is under attack.

It is no longer a question of "if the foundation be destroyed"—because it is being systematically dismantled and destroyed. It is now a question of "what can the righteous do?"

ENDNOTE

1.   Mark Christian, M.D., "Islamic Society: The Agent of Jihad in America," *World Net Daily,* July 28, 2015, http://www .wnd.com/2015/07/islamic-society-the-agent-of-jihad-in-america/.

CHAPTER 12

WHAT CAN THE RIGHTEOUS DO?

WHAT MORE COULD the disciples have done? Why stay awake? Why watch and pray? What is destined to be cannot be stopped, so why bother? What is our response to what is going on in the world today? There in the garden they stood watching helplessly as Judas betrayed Christ with a kiss. What were they to do? They were no match for the mob that followed him there. Some of them were barely awake, let alone able to absorb all that was taking place there in garden.

They had been given ample warning, and now they understood why Jesus had told them to watch. Three times He told them to watch and pray, yet Judas was able to walk right into the garden unhindered. We have been called upon to intercede, but Satan has entered into our garden, and we have done little to stop him. Where are the intercessors? Where are those whom God has placed on the perimeters of the garden as "watchmen" and people of prayer?

WATCH AND PRAY

Standing Between God and Sodom

In the eighteenth chapter of Genesis, we are shown the potential that is within our reach. We are shown what can happen if we will just wake up. It's the revelation of God to the church in the last days of America. In that great chapter God comes to Abraham and reveals His judgment that is about to befall Sodom and Gomorrah. Abraham would have missed his opportunity if he had not been in the tent door with his eyes open.

If ever there was a prophetic picture of the scene being played out in heaven at this very moment of time, this is it. And what a scene it is. The cry (shriek) of a wicked and perverse generation is coming up to God. His justice demands a response. I wonder if even now He is on His way to America to determine the level of punishment that will be brought to bear upon us. How full is the cup of iniquity in America?

There are three things that God showed me in this text that are noteworthy:

1. He personally delivers a blessing to Abraham.

2. God came to personally check out the situation before He judged the cities.

3. God hears and answers the prayers of the righteous.

The first solemn prayer in the Bible is found in this narrative; it was the prayer of Abraham in which he asked God to save Sodom if but a few righteous persons should be found in it. Come and learn from Abraham what compassion we should feel for sinners, and how earnestly we should pray for them.

We see here that the effectual, fervent prayer of a righteous man avails much (James 5:16). Abraham, indeed, failed in his request for the whole place, but Lot was miraculously delivered. Be encouraged then to expect, by earnest prayer, the blessing of God upon your families, your friends, your neighborhood.

To this end, you must not only pray, but you must live like Abraham. He knew the Judge of all the Earth would do right. He does not plead that the wicked may be spared for their own sake—or because it would be severe to destroy them—but he prays for the sake of the righteous who might be found among them. And righteousness only can be made a plea before God.

Abraham belonged to that select company of God's people known as intercessors— individuals like Moses, Samuel, Elijah, Jeremiah, the apostles, and our Lord Himself. In fact, our Lord's ministry today in heaven is a ministry of intercession (Rom. 8:34); so we are never more like our Lord than when we are interceding for others. It is not enough for us to be a blessing to our Lord and our home; we must also seek to win a lost world and bring sinners to the Savior.

Regarding intercession Charles Spurgeon said:

> If they [lost sinners] will not hear you speak, they cannot prevent your praying. Do they jest at your exhortations? They cannot disturb you at your prayers. Are they far away so that you cannot reach them? Your prayers can reach them. Have they declared that they will never listen to you again, nor see your face? Never mind, God has a voice which they must hear. Speak to Him, and He will make them feel. Though they now treat you despitefully,

rendering evil for your good, follow them with your prayers. Never let them perish for lack of your supplications.[1]

The Lord and the two angels left Abraham's camp and started toward Sodom, but the Lord lingered while the angels went on (Gen. 18:16, 22; 19:1). Abraham is now standing reverently before the Lord and interceding for Lot and the other people in Sodom. He is literally standing between God and Sodom.

An intercessor must know the Lord personally and be obedient to His will. He must be close enough to the Lord to learn His "secrets" and know what to pray about (Amos 3:7; Ps. 25:14). The Lord's words, "I know him" (Gen. 18:19), mean "I have chosen him, and he is My intimate friend" (see John 15:15). Abraham knew more about Sodom's future than the citizens themselves, including Lot. It is the separated believer who shares God's secrets.

Sarah and the servants helped Abraham when he prepared a meal for the three visitors, but when it came to the ministry of intercession, Abraham had to serve alone. Abraham drew near to the Lord (James 4:8), and the Hebrew word means "to come to court to argue a case." Abraham was burdened for Lot and Lot's family, as well as for the lost sinners in the five cities of the plain, and he had to share that burden with the Lord.

Abraham's prayer was based not on the mercy of God but on the justice of God. "Shall not the Judge of all the earth do right?" (Gen. 18:25). A just and holy God could not destroy righteous believers with wicked unbelievers; and Lot was a believer, even though his actions and words seemed to belie the fact.

The cities of Sodom and Gomorrah were exceedingly wicked because the men of these cities were given over to sexual practices that were contrary to nature. The words *sodomy* and *sodomize* are synonyms for these homosexual practices. The men did not try to hide their sin, nor would they repent. The sudden destruction of Sodom and Gomorrah is used in Scripture as an example of God's righteous judgment on sinners, and Jesus used it as a warning for people in the end times.

But why would Abraham want God to spare such wicked people? Far better that they should be wiped off the face of the Earth! Of course, Abraham's first concern was for Lot and his family. In fact, Abraham had already rescued the people of Sodom solely because of Lot, though none of the citizens seemed to appreciate what he had done for them. They all went right back into the old way of life and did not heed the warning of God.

But even apart from Lot's situation (and he should not have been in Sodom in the first place), Abraham did not want to see all those people die and be lost forever. God is "not willing that any should perish," and He "will have all men to be saved" (2 Pet. 3:9); 1 Tim. 2:4). God tells us, "I have no pleasure in the death of the wicked, but that the wicked turn from his way and live" (Ezek. 33:11). The issue is not what kind of sins people commit, though some sins are certainly worse than others, but that "the wages of sin is death," and beyond that, death is an eternal hell (Rom. 6:23). Intercessors must have compassionate hearts and a deep concern for the salvation of the lost, no matter what their sins may be.

We must not get the idea that Abraham argued with the Lord because he did not. He was very humble before the Lord as he presented his case (Gen. 18:27, 30–32). Abraham was sure that there were at least ten believers in the city. Never underestimate the importance of even a small number of believers. As few as ten people would have saved a whole city from destruction! If Lot had won only his own family to faith in the Lord, judgment would have been averted. Your personal witness today is important to God, no matter how insignificant you may feel.

WHAT'S THE USE?

What is the use? Why did Jesus have the disciples pray? What was going to be done would happen regardless, right? We will never know how things may have turned out because the will of God was not completely fulfilled in the disciples.

Jesus had strategically placed them in the garden. He had positioned eight of them on the outer perimeter of the garden (Matt. 26:36), and the other three within a stone's throw of Himself (Luke 22:41). When He told the eight to sit "here," Jesus was saying, "This is the spot that I want you to occupy." The same word is used for the placement of Peter, James, and John. Please don't overlook this point. God has positioned you and me at this strategic place in time. He knows what your abilities are. He knows your strengths and weaknesses. You are not a liability to Him. None of the disciples were a liability; though different in every way, each had a job to accomplish.

Abraham had taken up a strategic position on the mountains above Sodom so that he could intercede for them. Likewise, we must take our place in this moment of time to intercede on behalf of both our nation and the nation of Israel. God has entrusted you and me with the kingdom of heaven on Earth. We are living in the climax of the church age. We have been given charge over the greatest hour, but indeed it is also the most dangerous hour. What will we do with that which God has placed upon us?

Why did Jesus put them where He put them? I have to believe that none of the disciples were placed in their position randomly. I don't think God does anything randomly, so certainly He had a strategy. The command was clear: "Watch and pray"; the place was clear: "Here." Perhaps I am making too much of this. Maybe we just "happened" to be born when and where we were—or maybe "God has brought us to the kingdom for such a time as this" (see Esther 4:14).

Let's take a moment and look at the divine placement. Throughout the scriptures we see the right people, in the right place. In Queen Esther's situation, there was no other way to see it than divine placement (Esther 4:14). Her story fits this hour in more ways than one can imagine. When the prime minister of Israel was preparing to come to America to speak to Congress in the spring of 2015, he began drawing from Esther's story as an illustration of the seriousness of the hour.

The Jewish festival of Purim is celebrated every year in early spring to commemorate the Jewish rise against the Persian Empire. Israeli Prime Minister Benjamin Netanyahu invoked the Jewish Purim holiday during his speech before the U.S. Congress, citing the biblical deliverance of Jews from genocide under ancient Persian Empire rule and calling attention to the story of a Jewish girl named Esther, who rose to become Queen of Persia. "A courageous Jewish woman, Queen Esther, exposed the plot and gave for the Jewish people the right to defend themselves against their enemies," Netanyahu said of the Jews' salvation story as recounted in the Hebrew Bible or the Christian Old Testament. "The plot was foiled, our people were saved. Today the Jewish people face another attempt by yet another Persian potentate to destroy us."[2]

According to the Bible, during the time of King Ahasuerus, Haman, a minister to the king, sought to annihilate the empire's Jews in retaliation for being insulted by a Jewish man named Mordecai. The man learned of Haman's plan for retaliation and warned his cousin Esther, who had become queen of the empire, but whose Jewish identity had been kept secret. On the thirteenth day of the Hebrew month of Adar, following several days of fasting and prayer, the Jews rose up against their enemies and were victorious.

"But Iran's regime is not merely a Jewish problem, any more than the Nazi regime was merely a Jewish problem," Netanyahu told Congress. "The 6 million Jews murdered by the Nazis were but a fraction of the 60 million people killed in World War II. So, too, Iran's regime poses a grave threat, not only to Israel, but also the peace of the entire world. To understand just how dangerous Iran would be with nuclear weapons, we must fully understand the nature of the regime."[3]

It is with this "regime" that America now finds herself engaged. Judas is presently building relationships with those who are bent on the destruction of Israel. Like Haman in the story of Queen Esther, there are those who are determined to annihilate Israel, and they are the ones with whom our government is meeting. Through a time of fasting and prayer, Israel was able to turn the tide against Haman. They accepted their divinely appointed position and did what they had to do. Will the church in America do the same? Is there not a cause?

Why did Jesus place the majority of His disciples on the perimeter? Were they to be the first line of defense against those who were coming? We know that none of them had a sword, so they were not there to fight in the natural sense.

If they were not there to fight, what was the reason for their positioning? We know the primary reason they were in the garden with Him was to watch and pray. Could it be that Jesus had positioned them there so that in a sense they could give warning to Jesus of the approaching enemy? The word *watch* as it used in this text means watch with "vigilance and expectancy." It is the same word that is used in 1 Peter 5:8: "Be sober, be vigilant; because your adversary the devil, as a roaring lion, walketh about, seeking whom he may devour." Can't you hear the Lord saying this to the disciples as they were entering the garden? "Be vigilant, men; stay alert because your adversary the devil is walking around out there. He wants to come in here to devour. Are you going to let him in?"

Are we going to miss our assignment to watch and pray? Have we lost our sense of expectancy? Was their role like the biblical role of the trumpeters of Israel? Trumpets were used often to call for an assembly of the congregation, *direct* the movement of the camps, or *announce* the beginning of months or appointed feasts. They were also used to mobilize the army.

Where are the modern-day trumpeters? In Numbers 11:29, Moses said, "Would God that all the LORD's people were prophets, and that the LORD would put his spirit upon them!" It is only conjecture when we wonder why

Jesus positioned the disciples as He did, but I know this much, He didn't put them there to sleep. He didn't point out a place where the ground was softer than any other place in the garden. He didn't say, "Sit here, guys; this looks like a great place for you to take a break." He didn't point out a spot where they had a nice view of city walls so they could admire the beautiful city of Jerusalem in the moonlight. No, He put them there to pray and watch!

You were not brought to this moment to look for a nice place to retire. That is not to say that we should not take care of the necessities in our lives. One has rightfully said, "We are to live like He is coming any moment and plan like it will be forever." We must live with sobriety and vigilance in this, the closing moments of time. America is on the verge of betrayal. It is no small matter; this is life and death. Blow the trumpet, men and women of God. Preach like a dying man to a dying generation.

If they were not there to fight, what was the reason for their positioning? If they were not there for their own security, were they there for His? It was not possible that they could have stopped the treasonous act of Judas. No, this was all the plan of God. Each of the disciples had a God-given mandate, of that I am certain. So what was it?

Is it possible that God had brought them to this moment to protect them? We know that much of Jesus' time in prayer was for the disciples. We know that He came to check on them on three occasions. Did Jesus rebuke them? Yes. Did He wake them up? Yes. There is no question that His love for them is part of the reason for bringing them with Him. But was there more?

Were they there as a "buffer" against the enemy? Were they strategically placed so as to offer a sense of security?

If so, how could these eleven bring any level of security to the Son of God? What could they possibly do to help or strengthen Him? After all, they had a pretty dismal track record when it came to being strong for anyone, let alone in the face of an armed mob. When the ship was being tossed, they didn't have enough faith to let Him sleep—so why would this storm be any different?

We may never know why they were each in that particular place in the garden, but if it was to be a support to the Master, it didn't go so well. They had a willing spirit, but they were ruled by their flesh. So it is with the modern church. We have been given a divine directive to be sober and vigilant, yet it seems we are more interested in blessings and rest. Certainly we have been told to pray for Israel and the peace of Jerusalem. We know there is a kingdom connection between us and our Jewish brethren. We also know that there is an enemy that desires their destruction; that enemy is marching on her doorstep even now.

Our president is on the verge of betrayal. God forbid. We are only a few short days from witnessing the kiss that seals our place in history with so many other countries that were once rulers of the world. Haman is building his gallows; Hitler is building another Auschwitz; and as a roaring lion, Satan is seeking whom he may devour. Will we sit by while the gallows are constructed? Will we turn the other way while the smoke billows from the chimneys where the bodies burn? Will we repeat the history that allowed the Nazi death camps to exist? Or will we, like Esther, fast and pray? I choose the latter.

God has called Israel His son, so that makes us brothers. The church must become an ardent supporter of Israel. We are called to strengthen our brother and to be a guardian of Israel. We are called to watch and pray.

ENDNOTES

1. Charles H. Spurgeon, *The Metropolitan Tabernacle Pulpit*, vol. *18* (London: Banner of Truth Trust, 1969), 263–264.

2. "The Complete Transcript of Netanyahu's Address to Congress," *The Washington Post,* March 3, 2015, http://www .washingtonpost.com/news/post-politics/wp/2015/03/03/full-text -netanyahus-address-to-congress/.

3. Ibid.

CHAPTER 13

THAT YOUR FAITH FAILS NOT...

J ESUS AROSE FROM prayer and went to the three who were supposed to be praying with Him, only to find them fast asleep. The companionship, spirit of prayer, and comfort He had sought was not there. All were asleep, and as the Prophet Isaiah had declared, "He must walk the winepress alone" (see Isa. 63:3).

Christ warned of temptation. The disciples had failed to pray for Him, but they must not fail to pray for themselves. Christ said, "Watch and pray." Both were important. Watchfulness sees and praying prepares. They were to watch in order to see temptation coming, and they were to pray in order to be prepared when temptation struck. Christ warned of the flesh and its weakness. They were sleeping because of the emotional strain and distress of the evening. As Luke says, they slept because of sorrow, that is, sadness (Luke 22:45). The evening had been shocking and taxing. They were weary, fatigued, and preoccupied. Concentration in prayer was difficult. They probably fought to stay awake and pray for their Lord. But the importance of prayer and spiritual dependency upon God in facing trials had not yet been learned.

According to Luke's Gospel, Jesus had told His disciples on two occasions what it was they were to pray for. He said to them in Luke 22:40, 46 to pray that they enter not into temptation. What temptation was it that they were susceptible to? What temptations are we dealing within the church in America? The eyes of the disciples were heavy, and their hearts were weary. When a person is weary, they are more prone to the enemy's attack. There are many within the church who are weary. There are many who are struggling with heavy eyes.

Countless times I have found myself so tired that even though my eyes were open, my mind was numb. I have driven many miles without remembering anything about the drive—unable to remember road signs or any specifics about the journey. There is nothing scarier than arriving somewhere and wondering how you got there. There is nothing like that jolt back to reality as you hear the rumble strip on the edge of the highway or the sound of impact.

Not once, but on three different occasions, the disciples were awakened. It was not a gentle nudge, but the strong solemn words of Jesus that startled them. How did it happen? How did they go back to sleep? Peter certainly felt at his side to make sure that his sword was in its sheath. It seemed strange having a sword; after all, he was not a soldier and never had been. He was a fisherman. Carrying a sword was not likely his forté, and yet here he was in the garden on the night of the betrayal. He was the only thing that stood between Jesus and those who were bent on doing Him harm.

There was no way he was going to let someone hurt Jesus. There was no way he would deny Him even if he had to fight; he was ready. He had made a commitment to Jesus, and if it meant fighting to the death, that is exactly what he intended to do. It is so simple to make promises of devotion when there is no threat. Only a few hours earlier, he assured Jesus that nothing could possibly come between them—and now this.

He heard the tone in the Master's voice. It was different; he had never heard anything that compared to it. It wasn't that Jesus was afraid or nervous. None of that comes through in any of the narratives of the events that happened there in the garden. What was it then?

There was a deep sense of foreboding there in the garden. Perhaps that sense was present because the disciples had been so sound asleep and were suddenly awakened. Either way, there was a tangible uneasiness at work in the garden that night. I'm sure that neither their eyes nor their hearts were ready for what they were about to witness. There were flickering torches moving down the hill toward them. Someone was coming, but this was no surprise to Jesus. He had been awake. The ones who were caught off guard were the ones who should have been the first to see it.

Suddenly the night sky was on fire as men with torches and swords and clubs seemingly covered the entrance to the garden. Worst of all, they were led by one of their own. They were being led there by Judas. Is this what Jesus had warned them of? "Satan hath desired to have you, that he may sift you as wheat" (Luke 22:31). He was telling them something that you and I in the twenty-first century need to pay attention to as well. While we are focusing on our place of power and prestige, Satan is plotting our destruction. Jesus was saying to them, "Your distraction will become your destruction."

Satan wants to sift you; he wants to shake you and destroy you. His plan is the same today as it was then, yet we have become ignorant of his devices. Or is it possible that we are too familiar with his "vices" to see his devices? The word *sift* is *siniazo* in the Greek, and it means to separate and scatter. A sieve is shaken, and the shaking action separates and scatters. That was the devil's plan then, and it is his plan now. He knows that he can't destroy the church unless he can divide the church.

The disciples were getting ready to go through a sifting process, and the intended goal was to separate, scatter, and ultimately destroy them. What was the answer? Jesus said to Simon Peter, "But I have prayed for you, that your faith fail not!" (Luke 22:32). What is the Lord is trying tell us in this hour of betrayal? He is telling us to be aware of our enemy and keep our faith strong. This is the victory that overcomes the world, even our faith! (1 John 5:4).

"Satan desires to have you, but I have prayed for you!" While it is important for us to be aware of the enemy, he should never be our focus. There is a shaking that is coming, and only that which cannot be shaken will remain. The church is about to walk into some darkness, but God is in control.

What happened there in the garden is a very unfortunate picture of the church. When the adversary steps into the sanctuary, there has to be a plan of action. Had the disciples followed the directives of the Master, their minds would have been alert and their spirits would have been unified. As it was, they were numb. They were caught off guard. Their eyes burned from lack of sleep; no doubt their minds were fuzzy, and before they could absorb what was coming, it was over.

Often in traumatic situations a person's mind seems to kick things into slow motion. Even in slow motion it would have been difficult to wrap your brain around what was happening. The next few moments in the garden were nothing less than pandemonium. The act of betrayal, the guards, the mob, the sword—it seemed like the wheels had come off and everything was spinning out of control.

In spite of what it seemed like, everything was moving according to plan. From the perspective of the disciples it was chaos, but from Christ's vantage point, there was no confusion. This was the hour for which He had come. This was the darkness that He had come to shatter. He was in full control. Not Judas, not the Sanhedrin, not the guards. Jesus was in control.

As we are witnessing prophecy unfold and the unraveling of the relative tranquility of the nations, it is of vital importance that we realize how "in control" things are. Remember Paul's warning from 2 Thessalonians 2:2 when he tells us not to be shaken in the chaos of the last days. If the disciples had followed His directions, if they had listened in the Upper Room, they would have heard Him describe in detail the things that were coming. They would have known that the events unfolding in the garden were of His choosing. If they had prayed, they would have been spiritually prepared for what was happening. If they had stayed awake, they would have seen it coming.

Haven't we been given ample warning of the things that are happening in front of us? Not only do we have the words of the prophets and the disciples, but God is speaking through countless men and women today. There is no reason for the church to be unaware or off guard. God is not the author of confusion. He wants us to be at peace regarding the events of the last days.

> Peace I leave with you, my peace I give unto you: not
> as the world giveth, give I unto you. Let not your
> heart be troubled, neither let it be afraid.
>
> —JOHN 14:27

Unfortunately, the failures of the disciples are being played out yet again in the church. We are so preoccupied with personal kingdoms and thrones that we have not listened to Him. He has warned us countless times that the "kingdoms of this world are become the kingdoms of our Lord" (Rev. 11:15). No earthly throne lasts forever; every nation will have its Waterloo.

God showed King Nebuchadnezzar in the Book of Daniel a great vision. He showed him great nations who would rule the world. In that vision, he saw nations and kingdoms come and go. At last he saw another kingdom. It was a kingdom that belongs to one who was a stone that was "cut out of the mountain." That stone is Christ, and He will crush all nations, kings, and kingdoms.

No leader can out-maneuver Him. No one can outlast Him. The president of the United States is being maneuvered and manipulated by the same spirit that worked in Judas. Like Judas, Mr. Obama is in for a rude awakening. Things aren't going to go as he has planned. What seems like power today will be destruction tomorrow for those who are blinded by pride. You can't fight God, and you can't destroy His church. You may turn your back on Israel and walk hand in hand with those who want to destroy them, but Israel belongs to God, and He will take care of them.

Woe to those who have determined evil upon Israel! Woe to those who partner with the adversary! The actions of Judas had a severe affect on everyone, but none suffered more than Judas himself. His destruction did not end. Judas was nothing more than a tool that Satan found to get to Jesus. Likewise, those who are being used of the enemy need to understand how insignificant they are without the touch of God on their life.

The confusion that is about to be unleashed on America is unlike anything that we have ever seen. How the coming storm will affect the church, however, is still to be determined. I see within the framework of this prophetic word an important insight to how things will play out for the church. There are several individuals that I want to look at, and each of them is represented in the body of Christ today. In the next few chapters, I will deal with them in detail, but for now, let me remind you of the rapidity of the implosion that night in the garden.

Let's take a moment and play out the scene: The disciples were jolted to reality by Jesus. While He is speaking, the mob arrives on the scene. Judas leans in to kiss Jesus, and the guards fall as Jesus declares who He is. Peter pulled his sword from its sheath and cut the ear off of Malchus, the high priest's servant—and then Jesus heals the ear. When the guards seize Jesus, Mark tells us that every one of them forsook Him and fled. In the chaos and confusion of the moment, one of the guards grabbed Mark. In an effort to save his own life, he pulled himself free from the guard and ran off naked.

Judas, who only a few hours earlier had communion with Christ, is now left holding the bag. He stands there in silence and confusion. The mob is gone, the torch lights have faded, and the disciples are scattered. It probably took no more than ten minutes for everything to completely and totally blow apart.

When judgment falls on America, it is going to be swift. When God removes His hand of protection and favor from our nation, we are going to experience a shaking unlike anything that has happened heretofore. We are approaching that midnight hour. Are you prepared for the coming storm? What is the condition of the church in light of the forecast? Will we be found praying or sleeping? Are we watching, or are we too self-absorbed to see what is happening?

The disciples had succumbed to the temptations presented to them. They truly failed in their assignment to be watchmen on the wall. The night had come much more quickly than they could have imagined. With blistering speed, they had watched it all come crashing down around them.

CHAPTER 14

THE TORMENTED BETRAYER

*If thou hast run with the footmen, and they
have wearied thee, then how canst thou con-
tend with horses? and if in the land of peace,
wherein thou trustedst, they wearied thee, then
how wilt thou do in the swelling of Jordan?*
—JEREMIAH 12:5

BEFORE WE LOOK deeper into the situation that the disciples found themselves in, I want to look one more time at Judas. What Judas felt after his house of cards came crashing down is what America will experience when we betray Israel.

The Word of God is very clear that Satan had entered into Judas, and in John's Gospel narrative, he tells us that Judas "stood with" the enemy. What must that have felt like? For the last three years, he has stood shoulder-to-shoulder with Christ, and now Judas stands with those who would crucify Jesus. Did he feel empowered as he stood there? What was going through his mind?

To fully understand the emptiness that comes with doing the devil's bidding one need look no further than the events that followed. Judas had cast his lot with the wrong team. They had what they wanted from him, and now he was no longer needed. They had no interest in his future, and there was no sense of partnership. He was a pawn and nothing more. Whatever part he played was now inconsequential.

They had Jesus in their grasp, and whatever happened to Judas was of no concern to them. He simply did not matter. What a fool he had been to think that somehow he would be lauded, honored, or considered important. He now found himself more alone than he could have imagined, and not just because there was no one in the garden with him. No, this was deeper than that.

The reality of what he had done was now beginning to sink in. He had thirty pieces of silver in his bag. He had the funds of the ministry of Jesus in his bag. He thought it would feel different than this. Where were the feelings of importance? Where were the emotions that he had felt as he led that mob only a few minutes earlier?

Scripture does not tell us how long he stood there. We are certain that he never brought the thirty pieces of silver back until after Christ had been condemned, so we can surmise that Judas carried the weight of the betrayal throughout the long night and a good portion of the following day.

How good it had felt when they first handed him that bag. The clanging of the coins was such a sweet sound to the ears of this man who was a thief. He had in his bag the best of both worlds. He held the finances of the Kingdom of God and the wealth of the religious leaders. Now the weight of the coins was more than his heart could bear. Satan had used him, and when he had served whatever purpose the devil needed, he was left broke and broken.

Like the drug addict who has spent everything that he has for the next high, only to find out that when the high has ended he is lower than he started, Judas was at the bottom of the barrel. The sweet sound of the coins became a torment to him. The weight of them was more than he could bear. Through the long night he carried the burden of his betrayal. Rather than feeling better at daylight, the darkness only increased. I'm not sure what he was after. I don't know what he thought betrayal would bring or what it would feel like. Whatever his thoughts may have been, they were far from reality. Isn't that the way it goes? The enticement, the allure, the attraction is always an illusion.

America, please hear God calling you to repentance. Please hear the cry of the prophets calling you. Mr. Obama, please heed the warnings. History is full of the testimonials of leaders who have sat where you now sit. Ask Pilate if it was worth it to turn Christ over to His accusers. Ask Pharaoh if it was worth it. Your kingdom will meet the same fate as his. The waters of the Red Sea came crashing in. There is a tidal wave of destruction that is awaiting America.

The Red Sea is littered with chariot wheels that serve as a reminder that you can't touch God's people without suffering the ramifications. You don't have to go very far back in history to realize how dark it is for those who fight against Israel. There is certain calamity awaiting any nation that aligns itself with Satan.

Every president has sought to leave a legacy. What will be the legacy of Barack Hussein Obama? Will he be known as the man who fundamentally changed America? If so, what will that change look like? Again, one need only look at the failures of the past to see what awaits us in the future. The passion for power is driving him to do things that are jeopardizing our national security and future.

Look at Judas, Mr. Obama. Ask him what it felt like to betray Jesus. Look at his legacy. He is not recognized for his financial prowess or wisdom. No one honors him for the good that he accomplished. He fundamentally changed history, and that change brought about his demise.

Once we have empowered Iran to develop nuclear weapons we will have opened Pandora's box. There will be no turning back; the darkness unleashed on us will be immense. Those who gave the silver to Judas never disguised their desires. They never insinuated that they wanted any more or less than the death of Jesus. There was no way that he could have thought differently about the situation. The same could be said about President Obama's negotiations with Iran. They have never hidden their desires. They have always been forthright in their goals and ambitions. They seek the annihilation of God's chosen people. God calls Israel "my son" in Exodus 4:22. To sign an agreement with Iran is to become an accessory to murder. To assist them in this attempt to develop nuclear power is to not only kiss Israel with a betrayer's kiss, but to lead the march to the betrayal. We must choose which side we are going to line up on.

I cannot imagine the darkness that surrounded Judas there in the garden. The silence had to have been deafening. That is what is awaiting those who would betray Israel. Will Mr. Obama lead us into this dark valley? Will the church allow it to happen? We cannot separate ourselves from the ramifications of his actions. Whatever he does affects us as well.

When I asked God to judge our leaders but spare our nation, I was very sincere. I grieve at the thought of the coming judgment. Likewise, when I felt the Lord say that He could not judge the leaders and spare the nation because it was the nation that chose the leaders, I felt an equally heavy weight. What shall we do in the "swelling of the Jordan"? What becomes of the nation that breaks covenant with God and sells out His people?

Judas had a change of mind, but it was too late. He didn't change his mind until Jesus had been condemned. If America survives long enough, she will witness the events of Ezekiel 38–39. We will watch as the armies of the North, along with Iran, attack Israel with nuclear weapons. The Bible says that there will be those in the nations of the world who will ask Iran, "Why are you doing this?" No one stops them. No one stands up to them as they attack and attempt to wipe Israel off of the map. No one, that is, except God. Chapter 39 says that God will knock their arrows out of the sky and the bow out of their hand. God will get the credit and not man.

When people ask about America in Bible prophecy, all that any of us can say is this: "If America survives, she will be powerless." What a far cry from the place we find ourselves in presently. If America implodes, what does that mean for us? If God further removes His protective hand from our nation what will we look like? In the hours that followed Judas' betrayal of Christ, we see a glimpse into the final hours of the nation of America. Gone were the days of power and dominance. The good old days were a distant memory.

I remember the economic crash of 2008. We watched as business after business closed their doors. Unemployment and foreclosure ruled the headlines. We as a nation were in a free fall. In the local area where I live, one was hard pressed to find a used car lot, as one by one they shut their doors. No one was buying anything new because of the fear of another round of layoffs or shutdowns. The implosion that is coming to America as we continue this suicidal mission with Iran is much worse than anything we can imagine.

Judas waited until Jesus was condemned, and then he tried to make things right. The money he had been paid was used to purchase his own grave. God save America from this judgment. Furthermore, the Bible says Judas was repentant, but it doesn't say that he was forgiven. Sorry, yet condemned. We are told that Judas committed suicide by hanging himself. The act of suicide ended there, but it had begun the day before. When Judas walked out on Jesus, he was on borrowed time.

When America began this march to a two-state solution, when we began negotiating with the Supreme Leader of Iran, we began the act of suicide. Will we be resurrected from that death to someday reign again as a superpower? Or will we, like Judas, end up empty and broken, feeling the weight of our betrayal? Judas died broke. He died friendless. He died in torment.

I believe the reason that you don't find America in prophecy is because of the betrayal and the ramifications of such an act. We will be so decimated by either natural disasters, terrorist attacks, or financial collapse that we will become a nonplayer.

According to a recent Fox News report, ISIS claims to have terror cells in at least 15 states.[1] Homeland security has said, "It's not a matter of if they will attack, but when."

God warned Israel that He would appoint terror over them if they ever rejected Him. Certainly we are witnessing that in America as well.

The certainty of a catastrophic natural disaster cannot be overstated. Whether one is talking about an earthquake along the San Andreas Fault, the potential for a cataclysmic volcanic eruption in Yellowstone, or a major earthquake along the New Madrid Fault Line, one thing is clear, the big one is going to happen. When it does, it will change the face of America as we know it.

The coming financial crisis has most economists living on the edge of their seats. There is a feeling among many of the top financial strategists that we are approaching a time of total financial collapse. As of the 24th of June 2015, our debt is $18,156,514,883,479.97. The estimated population of the United States is 320,848,319; so each citizen's share of this debt is $56,589.09. The National Debt has continued to increase an average of $2.10 billion per day since September 30, 2012!

We often hear about the national debt, but the United States has an even bigger problem looming in the future: our unfunded liabilities. Unfunded liabilities is money that, under current law, the United States is scheduled to spend over its income. These include pensions for Federal employees, Medicare and Medicaid expenditures, and Social Security for future retirees. Those figures as of 2013 were estimated to be about $520 trillion. This is a hole we cannot dig our way out of. We can't print money fast enough to solve this dilemma. What is the answer? God is still in control, and if we will call upon Him, He can heal our land.

Perhaps I sound like a doomsayer. Friend, we as a nation are in deep trouble. The last thing that we need is to invoke the wrath of God. If one could somehow change every other aspect of our predicament; if there were no pending eruptions, earthquakes, hurricanes, or any number of potential natural disasters; if suddenly the terrorists of the world decided to ask our forgiveness and lay down their weapons; if all of our economic woes were to suddenly vanish and we were to start off on a clean slate; we would still be in trouble. Why? Because the greatest threat to our nation is a sin problem.

We have sinned against God, and we are rotting from the inside out. To add insult to injury we are now in the process of invoking His wrath by leading the enemy of Israel to them and betraying Israel with a kiss. When I use that phrase, I am merely saying that under the ruse of friendship we are betraying that relationship. If they were our enemies, we could never get that close, but because they are "friends," we can approach them in such a manner.

Little by little we are betraying that friendship. Just as Judas used his friendship to get close to Jesus, we have used ours to pinpoint Israel's most strategic weapons programs. In January 2015, the United States decided to release photos and details of Israel's nuclear weapons facility. While we have details of countless other countries' sites, we only released the details on the Israeli sites. It seems odd that we would reveal these long-held secrets, doesn't it? It was reportedly a part of our revenge for Benjamin Netanyahu coming to America to meet with Congress. In an effort to teach him a lesson, America revealed long-held secrets that ultimately affect Israel's security.

America has begun the process of selling out our friend. Against all conventional wisdom, we continue our meetings with Iran. The concessions that we have agreed to not only serve to undermine our position as the world's "superpower," but also place the nation of Israel in a precarious position. Furthermore, by strengthening the regime in Iran we are destabilizing the entire Middle East. Now Iran is using our apparent weakness to expand their agenda. It is an agenda that not only includes the whole of the Middle East, but also the United States.

Only time will tell the level of betrayal that is coming or that which has already taken place, but you can be certain the ultimate betrayal is coming. While we can fill in the blanks based on what is being released by the news media regarding our negotiations with Iran, we cannot imagine the long-term damage that will be done. It is more than propping up a regime; it is more than allowing the atrocities of Iran to go unchecked. It isn't even about trying to build bridges with Iran. The real issue is that we know exactly who it is that we are dealing with, and we know what they are going to do. Our ongoing negotiations with Iran are tantamount to supplying bricks for the ovens of Auschwitz. "For he that biddeth him God speed is partaker of his evil deeds" (2 John 1:11).

We have been warned by God in 1 Chronicles 16:22 to "touch not mine anointed." No one has ever prospered who had a part in the cursing of Israel. In Numbers 22–24, we find Balak, the king of the Moabites, who was afraid of Israel and tried to bribe the prophet Balaam to curse Israel. But when Balaam saw Israel camped in the wilderness, God spoke to him these words: "You cannot curse Israel; they are blessed." America must come to that realization if we are to see the mercy of God upon our land.

When Jesus had finished praying in the garden, an angel came and ministered to Him: "And there appeared an angel unto him from heaven, strengthening him" (Luke 22:43). God still has the ability to take care of His people Israel as He took care of His Son Jesus. He can send angels to minister to them; He has before, and He will again. God doesn't need America, but America certainly needs Him. Israel doesn't need America, but America definitely needs Israel. Why? When you embrace Israel, you are embracing their Father.

Throughout Scripture, we see God protecting Israel. Why would He do any less for them today?

> And it came to pass that night, that the angel of the LORD went out, and smote in the camp of the Assyrians an hundred fourscore and five thousand: and when they arose early in the morning, behold, they were all dead corpses.
> —2 KINGS 19:35

I believe God has allowed the United States of America to serve as protector to His people. When we turn our back on them, He will show His might on their behalf. He told Israel that their enemy would come in one way, but would flee seven ways.

MENE, MENE, TEKEL, UPHARSIN.

> This is the interpretation of the thing: MENE; God hath numbered thy kingdom, and finished it.

TEKEL; Thou art weighed in the balances, and art found wanting.

PERES; Thy kingdom is divided, and given to the Medes and Persians.
—DANIEL 5:24–28

Are our days numbered? Is America on borrowed time? As Judas watched the kangaroo court that condemned Christ, the weight of his betrayal became too much. Once Jesus was condemned and the devil was through with him, he felt the full impact of his actions. Judas could have found forgiveness for his actions. Instead of forgiveness and grace, Judas took the matter into his own hands and hanged himself. What a tragedy. He had gone from the highest of heights to the absolute lowest of lows in such a brief time. Matthew 26:24 says, "It had been good for that man if he had not been born."

Some have asked, "Why do you believe America will be judged more harshly than any other nation? Certainly there are more ungodly nations." Although there are many nations who are more ungodly than ours, no nation has walked as closely to the Lord as America has. In that regard, like Judas, we have fallen so much further.

Still others have suggested that there are many sins that are greater than turning our back on Israel. When you begin to list the many actions that we have taken to offend God, one could argue for the case of abortion being the most grievous sin. The fact that our nation has sanctioned and even blessed the slaughter of more than 56 million babies cannot be overlooked. If the blood of Abel cried out from the ground, what must the blood of nearly 60 million babies sound like?

Recently the Supreme Court sanctioned the marriage of homosexuals in America. By a 5 to 4 vote, they overrode the majority of America's votes and made homosexual marriage a constitutional right. Surely God does not look at that lightly. The actions of this judicial authority are not only illegal; they are unconscionable. America is sinking to all-new lows under President Obama. In the days following the tragic vote that rejected God's order, Mr. Obama ordered the White House to be lighted with the colors of the rainbow to celebrate the left's victory over God's law.

By embracing the sin of Sodom, America embraced the judgment that fell on Sodom. You cannot reject the principles of God and the order of nature without suffering the repercussions of those actions. Like Belshazzar in the Book of Daniel, America is rejoicing in the temple of self-indulgence. Belshazzar used the items that had been created for worship in the temple as instruments of his drunkenness. Today the wicked are using their bodies which were created in the image of God to fulfill their wicked desires.

The "Ultimate Party Crasher" is about to step on the scene, and the party is going to come to an abrupt end. Streets that have been filled with the perversion of the gay pride celebrations will overflow with the judgment of God. Recently I wrote that America must repent for voting for Barack Obama. I believe those who voted for him are complicit in his wicked acts that are destroying the fabric of our nation. An individual responded to the article, and the first words of her response are worth noting. "I will not repent!" She was involved in a homosexual relationship, and if there was even a possibility that she was committing sin, she was determined to live her way. Look at the words of Revelation 9:21: "Neither repented they of their murders, nor of their sorceries, nor of their fornication, nor of their thefts." Can't you hear the rebellion in that passage? That is the spirit that is ruling in this ungodly society today.

While each of these sins warrants divine retribution, there is nothing that demands the wrath of God as much as touching the apple of His eye. How long will the Lord wait to judge the wickedness of America? We do not know when, but there can be no question that His judgment is coming and that it will be swift. The streets of our cities will be filled with the sounds of lamenting mothers crying out for their children. Fires will light the skies of the inner cities of America as God unveils His holy fire upon this nation. In a matter of moments we will go from the most powerful nation on the planet to the most pitiful. There will, however, be no pity. We are quickly running out of time. America, like Judas, will find herself friendless, helpless, and hopeless.

The cup of the Lord's wrath is full! The handwriting is on the wall. Our days are numbered. We are weighed in the balance and found wanting. Judas, the treasurer of Christ's earthly kingdom, hanged himself. America is at the end of the rope, and life is quickly fading. We are taking our last gasp as we dangle so very close to the end. It is altogether possible that we will implode from the sheer weight of our sins. It is also possible that we will continue to exist as a nation for some time into the future. We will not simply disappear overnight, but it is doubtful that we will be what we are today. Our government is rushing toward the wrath of God.

Recently a member of Congress told me how frustrating it is to watch the nation rushing toward calamity. He expressed the futility of trying to turn America back to what our founding fathers designed it to be. One of his greatest concerns has been seeing our government's move toward Iran and away from Israel. He said, "No one can figure out why Mr. Obama is doing what he is doing. He is making decisions that make absolutely no sense. They fly in the face of conventional wisdom."

Is it possible that Mr. Obama is operating under a satanic anointing? Judas did, and it brought complete and utter destruction to him. Is it too late for America? Can the ship be turned around before it strikes the iceberg? It remains to be seen, but what we do know is this: "God is in full control, and He will be glorified!"

The wisdom of man will lead to absolute destruction, but when all is said and done, God will be glorified. There are things that are happening that are out of our control. It is one of the difficult things about where we are at this crucial moment in time. While we are directed to watch and pray, we are called upon to do more than watch and to do more than to pray. We must become actively involved in every aspect of our nation. As we see the end approaching, we must keep our eyes wide open and our hearts clean.

It remains to be seen whether a national revival can turn the tide or keep back the judgment of God. Had the disciples fulfilled their mandate in the garden, I'm sure things would have been different for them. Perhaps they would not have fled. Perhaps they would not have scattered like sheep without a shepherd. While we can only conjecture what it may have been like for the disciples, we dare not repeat their shortcomings.

ENDNOTE

1.   "Purported ISIS Warning Claims Terror Cells in Place in 15 States," *Fox News,* May 6, 2015, http://www.foxnews.com/us /2015/05/06/purported-isis-warning-claims-terror-cells-in-place -in-15-states/.

CHAPTER 15

THE NAKED DISCIPLE

And there followed him a certain young man,
having a linen cloth cast about his naked body;
and the young men laid hold on him: and he left
the linen cloth, and fled from them naked.
—MARK 14:51–52

THERE IS MUCH debate on who this individual was in Mark's Gospel. Some suggest that it was Lazarus or the rich young ruler, but many agree that it was Mark himself. Perhaps out of regret or modesty, he doesn't use the first person here, but that is not altogether uncommon. St. John nearly always referred to himself in the third person. Whoever it was, we know he was in the garden that night with the eleven, so it was most likely John Mark. This is likely the same Mark that Paul said he would rather not journey with in Acts 15:38.

Whether this was Mark or someone who was just caught up in the drama of the betrayal, we don't know. If it wasn't Mark, then it makes no sense to even tell the story, except to illustrate the confusion of the night. I am personally of the opinion that it was Mark because the word *follow* denotes to follow as a disciple.

It is one of the strangest stories in the whole of the narrative. In the chaos and confusion of the betrayal, the guards apparently are attempting to arrest anyone associated with Jesus. It is pandemonium in the garden as the disciples run for their lives. As one of the guards attempts to arrest him, Mark turns to run, and when he does, he literally runs out of his robe.

Some commentators believe that Mark ran back to his mother's house where they had previously gathered for the Last Supper. I wonder if he thought, "Since we are close to home, I might as well dress comfortably." I imagine he, like all of the others, missed the warnings that Jesus was giving. He missed the significance of both the Last Supper and the last night. Caught up in crowds and crowns, he failed to pay attention to Jesus. Now it was going to be an embarrassing situation. Now all would see just how unprepared he was. Perhaps he was used to late-night prayer meetings. Maybe he thought that it would be over soon and he would go back to his mother's house there in Jerusalem and go to bed. There was something about him that sounds eerily similar to many in the church today.

As we approach the end of the church age, there are many who are unprepared for what is ahead of us. We see no need to put on the whole armor of God; we just want to be comfortable. Unfortunately, the primary outcome of the "bless me" generation is that we are only one conflict away from realizing just how naked we are. Like the Laodicean church in Revelation 3:17, Jesus is warning us, "Because thou sayest, I am rich, and increased with goods, and have need of nothing; and knowest not that thou art wretched, and miserable, and poor, and blind, and naked." The Greek word for *naked* is *gumnos;* it means "to be naked; unclad; stripped of arms; defenseless." What a powerful word is used to describe them! When the soldiers lay hold of the disciple, they revealed how defenseless he really was.

I hear the Holy Spirit speaking to the church. He knows that we are headed toward the greatest shaking in our history. He knows that the enemy is going to attempt to capture the body of Christ. God is crying out to the unprepared church of the last day. I believe the Spirit is telling us that because of the tragic decisions of our president, we are going to find ourselves in unfamiliar territory. We cannot go into tomorrow acting like it was yesterday.

Mark looked as prepared as any of the others. He had taken time to put on the outer garment. If indeed the Passover supper had taken place at his home, did he take this opportunity to just relax a little? Perhaps he thought, "We will probably pray awhile, and then I'll come back home and get some rest." Whatever the case, he had certainly not been listening to the words of Jesus, or he would have dressed appropriately. This was not a time to relax. These were the last moments of the ministry of Christ. This was the hour of the betrayal. Whatever one had been able to do before, there was certainly no place for it now. There had to be a heightened sense of awareness. His cavalier dress was most likely a sign of his casual attitude. It is an attitude that is prevalent in the hour that we are living in. The church is lackadaisical in an hour when we can ill afford to be. We have let our guard down and are in danger of exposing our own nakedness.

The Laodicean Church stands as a stark reminder that how we see ourselves is not how God sees us. He has never been fooled by our outward appearance. Religious clothing only fools religious people. We take great care in things that matter little and little care in the things that matter greatly. Jesus stood outside of the Laodicean church. He was not involved in their self-absorbed services. The words spoken by Christ regarding this church could have been spoken to any one of thousands of the churches in America that are equally blinded to their own nakedness: "Because thou sayest, I am rich, and increased with goods, and have need of nothing" (Rev. 3:17a).

Let me put it in terms that you might hear today: "We have a positive confession. I am blessed; I am rich; I have all things that pertain to life. I am blessed and highly favored." Now, to be clear, there is nothing wrong with a positive confession. We should have a positive attitude and speak life and not death, but speaking life and failing to live a godly life will lead to destruction. Unfortunately, many times we live unbalanced lives. Our words declare that we are the righteousness of God in Christ Jesus, but our lives are loose. We are so focused on being increased with goods that we fail to see how empty we are.

Solomon gives us insight into what the scene of Revelation 3 may have looked like to Jesus as He stood on the church steps. The Song of Solomon is the love story between Christ and His church. In the fifth chapter, we are told just how desperately He longs to be with us as He stands at the door of His beloved and knocks. In this picture, Jesus does more than just knock; He calls out to His beloved. "Open to me, my sister," He says. "My love, my dove, my undefiled. Your eyes should be fixed upon me like mine are upon you; you are my undefiled church! Open to me! I have been standing here knocking so long that my hair is dripping with the dew of the night air! Open to me" (see Song of Songs 5:2).

What an insight into His determination for real fellowship with His bride: "I am come into my garden, my sister, my spouse: I have gathered my myrrh with my spice; I have eaten my honeycomb with my honey; I have drunk my wine with my milk: eat, O friends; drink, yea, drink abundantly, O beloved" (Song of Songs 5:1). How deep the pain His pain must be when we sit inside of our sanctuaries and respond in the manner described by Solomon: "I'm sleeping, I'm naked, and I don't want to get my feet dirty walking to the door" (see Song of Songs 5:3). "Behold I stand at the door and knock," says Christ (Rev. 3:20). His hands drip with the anointing, but we are missing it. How long will He knock before He walks away? When He walks, He takes His provision with Him. He is weary with our celebration services; He is tired of the church throwing a party in His honor but not inviting Him.

> I hate, I despise your feast days, and I will not smell in your solemn assemblies. Though ye offer me burnt offerings and your meat offerings, I will not accept them: neither will I regard the peace offerings of your fat beasts. Take thou away from me the noise of thy songs; for I will not hear the melody of thy viols. But let judgment run down as waters, and righteousness as a mighty stream.
>
> —Amos 5:21–24

The church would do well to heed the call of God. We need righteous streams to flow through our churches. He longs to release a torrent of His presence. When He does, much of what we call church will be washed away. He is saying, "Let Me in. I want to have communion with you; I have everything that you are looking for." Jesus is saying to the church, "I am everything you need!" May God awaken His church before it's too late. I am so glad that He is willing to continue knocking and calling.

From all of the outward signs, Mark the naked disciple looked like all of the others—the same robe, same sandals, same prayers (or lack thereof). When troubles come, they tend to reveal lack. It was the case with Mark, and it will be the case with the church in America. The church declares, "We are about to receive the greatest transfer of wealth in history." Is wealth really what is needed in the church? Do we really think that God will bless our mess? If God warned Israel that He was weary with their religion, and if He told the Laodiceans that He would "spew the lukewarm believers out of his mouth," why would He do any differently with us? (Rev. 3:16).

Friend, I am not a gloom-and-doom preacher. I am a prosperity preacher, but I have little interest in the prosperity that makes the church lethargic and ineffective. Wealth is not the answer to the church. Jesus told them so much when He said, "Take your money and buy gold that is tried in the fire. Take your money and buy some white raiment so your nakedness is covered" (see Rev. 3:18). The naked church grieves the Lord. He is crying out to us, "Cover the shame of your nakedness."

WHEN GOD REVEALS OUR NAKEDNESS

What revealed the nakedness of Mark? An attack of the enemy pulled the covering off. When the hand of God comes off of America, I am afraid that the American church will be found as naked as Mark was. The story of this naked disciple is interesting, isn't it? No other Gospel narrative tells the story. I have wondered why it is only found in the Book of Mark. Why tell of this event that quite honestly makes you look so ill prepared? The answer is simple. God allowed it to be revealed to show us how desperately we need to guard against our own nakedness.

Jesus had warned the disciples again and again, "This night is going to be different." It was going to be a night unlike any they had experienced in the past three-and-a-half years. His warning fell on deaf ears. Mark was so focused on his own comfort that he missed the warning.

We are living in a different hour in America. We are likely to see changes in the tax laws of America that will remove our tax-exempt status for not obeying the mandates to perform homosexual marriages. There are many who are attempting to institute hate crimes legislation that will criminalize the preaching of the Gospel when that message confronts the homosexual lifestyle. This is not just another night in Sodom! This is not just another day in the life of a nation! These are the final moments of society as we have known it. The robe is about to be pulled off. We are either prepared for what is coming or we are not. Our lack of preparedness will not change the reality of what is coming.

Jesus said to the leaders of Israel in His day what His Spirit is saying to us today, "You hypocrites, you can discern the natural weather but how is it that you do not discern this time?" (Luke 12:56). We have weather spotters and storm chasers who spend their lives watching to see what is coming. They put their lives in harm's way continually as they try to learn why weather patterns move the way they do. We know "jet streams" and "updrafts"; we know "tropical depressions" and "El Ninos," but we can't see the storm that is approaching in the spirit world.

The nakedness of the church is unparalleled in modern church history. We march so proudly in our religious garb, but like the religious leaders of Christ's day, we are whitened sepulchers full of death. When God shakes the nation, He will simultaneously judge the church. Judgment is about to begin, and this time it will be a multi-faceted judgment. God will judge this nation for its sinfulness. He will judge it for the attack on the unborn, and He will judge it for its embrace of the homosexual agenda. The greatest judgment is going to be connected to our embrace of Islam and rejection of Israel. Anything that is tied to the earthly will shake with it. Only those who are wholly living by the Spirit will be able to survive the coming storm.

In the betrayal of Christ, we find the unveiling of flesh. In one moment Mark looked like the rest of the disciples, and the next minute he was naked. How will we do when the enemy moves against the church? Will we fair better than Mark, or will our nakedness be revealed?

> For the time is come that judgment must begin at the house of God: and if it first begin at us, what shall the end be of them that obey not the gospel of God?
>
> —1 PETER 4:17

In the Garden of Eden, only God could cover the wickedness of man. The fleshly efforts of man are an affront to God. It takes the shedding of the blood of the innocent to cover the sin of the guilty. Mark was unprepared, and his lack was uncovered; the attack of the enemy revealed his real need. When the onslaught begins, may it bring each of us to our knees. May the judgment that is coming awaken us to our most desperate need. Jesus is standing at the door of His church. He sees us as His bride, His love, His beloved. He longs for genuine fellowship with His church. He longs to cover our nakedness and present us to the Father as His righteous bride, without spot or blemish.

We see the wall cloud of a coming storm. Our nation is in the path of the same storm that brought down so many others. When it hits, it will reveal our preparedness or lack thereof. The church is about to be uncovered.

THE STRIPPING AWAY OF OUR OUTER GARMENTS

God will allow the enemy to get close enough to reveal the true nature of His people. He doesn't do it out of anger. He does it because He knows that as long as the robe is there, we will try to hide behind it. The Lord of glory is about to allow the cover to be removed. Gone will be the self-righteous robes of religion. Gone will be the robes of fleshly motives and passions.

If the robe was taken from you, what would be revealed? Have you girded yourself with the truth of His Word?

> Let your loins be girded about, and your lights burning.
>
> —LUKE 12:35

What God considers important is not the same as what you and I do. He would rather you worship in Spirit and in truth. He longs for His bride to sanctify herself, to come out from among this world and be wholly His. He so desperately desires a true and sincere relationship that He is going to allow the removal of everything else.

CHAPTER 16

THE REPENTANT CHURCH

As you study the life of Peter, it is interesting to see the many dynamics of his life. He was unquestionably the most outspoken of the disciples and apparently had quite the attitude. He was one of the inner three of the disciples. When you see him, you will typically see James and John as well. While we could run through a list of events that he was a part of in Jesus' ministry, I want to focus my attention on the final moments there in the garden and beyond.

Peter, James, and John were hand selected by Christ to become His watchmen there in the depths of the garden. This was not their first time to be selected for an assignment, but it would certainly be the greatest. They had journeyed with Jesus to mountain of transfiguration, and they had heard the Old Testament prophets Moses and Elijah as they discussed with Jesus the events surrounding the cross. They were given a front-row seat for the event that all of heaven was watching. More than twelve legions of angels stood ready for Jesus' beaconed call. One angel was there in the garden with Jesus to minister to Him.

These three had the privilege to be just a short distance away from the place where heaven and Earth were about to collide. Merely a stone's throw away from them knelt the

King of glory. Just a stone's throw away the greatest battle in the history of the world was about to unfold. Jesus was preparing to confront not only the Cross, but the curse. In this garden, He would determine the destiny of humanity, and they were positioned perfectly to watch it unfold.

For more than three years, they had heard Jesus speak of this night. There was no excuse for their lack of preparation. For Peter, James, and John, this was as good as it gets. As the eldest disciple, Simon Peter probably felt a little more pressure. We are told of an instance in Matthew 16:21–23 when he had evidently gotten tired of hearing Jesus talk about His impending death. The Bible tells us that Simon Peter pulled Jesus aside and began to rebuke Him. Certainly Peter meant no harm by his concern for Jesus' well-being; he cared deeply for the Master and fully believed that Jesus was indeed the Son of God. Yet at his rebuke, Jesus became angry and cried out, "Get thee behind me, Satan!"

It was as though Jesus was looking past him, yet Peter understood that what he had told the Lord was summarily rejected: "But he turned, and said unto Peter, Get thee behind me, Satan: thou art an offence unto me: for thou savourest not the things that be of God, but those that be of men" (Matt. 16:23).

The events of the past couple of weeks were almost a blur in his weary mind. Only a week earlier, he had been overwhelmed by the welcome Jesus had received by the people of Jerusalem. It seemed like everyone in the city came out to celebrate the coming of the Messiah. Unlike other times, Jesus didn't stop them; He didn't slip out of town unnoticed as He had in the past. Perhaps Jesus was ready to accept His kingdom. Everything was going great;

Simon Peter now had the opportunity to witness the next step, whatever it was.

He couldn't help but wonder why Jesus questioned his dedication. After all, he was the one who had enough confidence in Jesus to walk on the water with Him. He had always shown unshakeable devotion to Him even when others mocked or walked away. Why would Jesus think that he of all people would betray Him? But that is exactly what He said, "Tonight you will betray me three different times."

As he knelt there in the garden contemplating the events of the past week, his mind began to drift. He could hear the conversations that filled the room. He could hear the question that was asked by the others, "Who will be the greatest?" This had been a source of contention; some strife rose up as they each began to state their case for a ranking position in the kingdom. Then there was the talk of betrayal again as Jesus said, "One of you will betray Me." Could Jesus be speaking of Peter? He had said in front of everyone that Peter would betray Him that night not once, but three times.

These thoughts and a million more swept over his mind and were as thick as the fog that had now begun to settle on the olive grove that night. He could hear Jesus praying, and he tried to focus on what was being said. There was something so beautiful about the way that Jesus prayed. At one point, they had even asked Him to teach them how to pray like that.

Jesus had told them to watch and pray, but it was so tough for Peter to clear his head. He knew he needed to pray, and he felt that this command to watch was equally important. How it happened and at what point in the night he didn't know. All he knew now was that he could hear Jesus talking. What had he missed? As he lifted his head, he realized that Jesus was indeed talking to him and the others. He was reprimanding them for going to sleep. Had he really gone to sleep? Unfortunately, he had, and so had all of the others. How could he do that? Was this the betrayal that Jesus had spoken of? Surely not. They had attended a lot of late-night prayer meetings, and surely there were times when they would nod off.

WAS IT THAT BIG OF A DEAL?

He would see to it that it never happened again, but it did, and again they were awakened by Jesus. As he listened to the Lord's prayer, he could hear a sense of deep burden. The compassion in the Master's voice was palpable. It seemed that the Father had come down to the garden with Jesus, and they were talking together. Before you know it, Peter again drifted off.

He was awakened again, but this time something was different. When his eyes finally got clear enough to see what was going on, he fixed them upon Jesus. He didn't know whether to apologize or how to express his deep sorrow for having let the Lord down; he just stared for a moment. His eyes looked upon the face of Jesus, only now His face was covered in blood. Had someone slipped in somehow and harmed the Master?

His thoughts were interrupted as Jesus spoke to them again. He said, "Get up. It's time to go. The one who will betray Me is coming." When the disciples turned to look in the direction that Jesus was looking, they couldn't believe their eyes. It looked like the whole Roman army was coming. Torches and clubs raised high, men with swords were marching down the hill directly toward them.

Peter could not believe his eyes. There at the front of the mob was Judas. What was going on? What was Judas doing with the high priest and the religious leaders?

Without saying anything to anyone else, Judas walked straight up to Jesus, called Him Rabbi and then kissed Him. Before he realized what was going on, Peter had taken the sword out of its sheath and aimed for the man nearest to him. He felt it make contact. He wasn't sure who he hit or where he hit him, but he wasn't going to allow them to take Jesus. If it meant dying for Him, that is what he was willing to do.

What he saw next caught him completely by surprise. Jesus stopped him dead in his tracks and quickly told him to put the sword back in its place. Then he watched the Lord reach over and heal the ear of the servant to the high priest. What was Jesus doing? This was not the time to heal; this was the time to kill. Then Jesus reprimanded him yet again, "If you live by the sword, you will die by it" (see Matt. 26:52).

Before he knew it, they were dragging Jesus away. The lights flickered in the dark as the mob moved off in the distance. Fear had swept through the hearts of the disciples, and they scattered. Every one of them ran; it seemed like some of them were running just to be running, having no sense of direction. Not Peter, he knew where he was going. He was going to follow Jesus; he would stay with the Master whatever that meant. There was no way he was going to let Jesus down. He had sworn his undying allegiance to Christ, and now with his hand on the sword he followed, keeping his distance to be sure.

LIVING BY THE SWORD

Simon Peter was ready to die for the cause. He proved that much there in the garden. Wherever they were taking Jesus, he was going to be. Why did everyone run away? The words of Jesus replayed again and again as he walked in the darkness of the Kidron Valley; "Put up again thy sword into his place: for all they that take the sword shall perish with the sword. Thinkest thou that I cannot now pray to my Father, and he shall presently give me more than twelve legions of angels?" (Matt. 26:52–53).

Peter's actions could certainly be considered a just use of defensive violence. Jesus, an innocent man, was about to be given into the hands of an angry mob. Using one of the swords Jesus had told him to buy, Peter had attempted to rescue his friend. Jesus, however, rebuked Peter and this use of defensive violence. Later at his trial before Pilate, Jesus made a comment which explained His condemnation of Peter's actions: "My kingdom is not of this world: if my kingdom were of this world, then would my servants fight" (John 18:36). If Jesus' kingdom were of this world, His servants could use defensive violence when attacked. However, Jesus' kingdom is not of this world. The rebuke was given to show you and me where our real strength lies.

Jesus didn't need Simon Peter to defend Him: "Don't you understand? I can call more than 72,000 angels to defend Me if I want, so quit living by the sword!" He wasn't telling Simon Peter not to carry a sword. Jesus simply said, "Don't try to use your sword to fight for Me." It is so important for the modern church to understand how futile our efforts are. I know of many individuals who have amassed an arsenal of weapons and ammunition. The question is often asked, "Is that right? Should Christians be prepared to defend themselves or their family?" Was Jesus telling Simon Peter that it is wrong to carry a weapon? The answer is no. He didn't tell him to quit carrying it; He said, "Put your sword back in its place."

To use the Lord's reprimand of Simon Peter as a reason for being against self defense would be erroneous at best. Presently in America we still enjoy the freedom of the Second Amendment, which guarantees us the right to keep and bear arms. That is a freedom that is constantly under attack by the socialists among us. There are many who would love nothing more than to confiscate our weapons. As a Christian, not only do I feel that it is my right to carry a weapon, but it is my responsibility to protect my family.

There is a lot of emphasis being placed upon preparation for the coming storm. There are many who are rightly called "doomsday preppers" because of their attempts to build fortifications and stockpile goods for the chaos that is coming. Over the past few years, there have been record numbers of Americans who are first-time gun buyers. Many times throughout President Obama's time in office, there has been a nation-wide shortage of ammunition. While he has not publicly attempted to ban guns in America, he has taken a very strong stand against gun ownership. Meanwhile, this fear of gun control along with many signs of an attempt to forego many provisions of the United States Constitution and the rights that are clearly defined within it is causing a tremendous sense of anxiety.

The feelings of trepidation that are prevalent in the nation are creeping into the church. Some of this is because of the continued attack on religious liberties from the executive and judicial branches of government. The Supreme Court has begun to write and rewrite laws that are changing every aspect of life as we know it. There is no balance of power, and with each executive order of the president, we are seeing less and less freedom.

Jesus told us in Luke 21:26 that a time was coming when men's hearts would fail them for fear as they watched what was coming on the Earth. That is not the plan that God has for His church. Jesus warned of terrible times; He warned us to not walk in fear of those times or of the things that are coming. He said in John 14:1, "Let not your heart be troubled." It is so easy to watch the news from around the world and here at home and become enraged by what you see. We cannot let what is taking place in the world move us from the place of peace wherein God has called us to walk. Neither can we afford to be ignorant of the danger that is breeding in our culture.

Recent church shootings remind us how important it is for churches to take necessary steps to secure their properties. There are those who believe that as long as you are "Spirit-filled," you don't need church security. I have heard them say things like, "If that pastor had been full of the Spirit of God, he wouldn't have been shot." That is as foolish as saying, "If Paul the Apostle had been Spirit-filled, he wouldn't have been beheaded." With the growing threat of ISIS as well as other rogue terrorist organizations, the church has to be on alert.

When you think of Simon Peter, it is easy to see the church of the last days. There are so many characteristics that are parallel to what is taking place today. Let's follow his journey from the betrayal to the resurrection.

Before the Cock Crows...

Simon Peter followed the mob back up across the Kidron Valley and on to the house of Annas and Caiaphas (see Matt. 26:58–75). It was the middle of the night, and there weren't many people on the streets at that time of the night. The guards were likely on high alert, and I'm sure everyone was a little nervous as they made their way to the Palace of the High Priest.

This was certainly not the safest place for Simon Peter to be given the events of the past couple of hours. His sword was likely stained with some of the blood from Malchus, who was probably there in the building if not in the same room. Possibly in an attempt to blend in or because he was nervous and cold, Peter found a seat close to the fire and tried to warm himself. While he was on the lower floor in the servants' area, Jesus was up in the hall being falsely accused by the high priest.

It was there, near the fire where Simon Peter was warming himself, that his first denial took place. A maiden of the high priest looked at him and accused him of being with Jesus; he refused to claim any relationship to Christ. No doubt under conviction for his denial and in attempt to get away from his accuser, Peter made his way to the porch. As he searched for some fresh air and tried to pull his thoughts together, he looked into the night sky. Another maiden approached him then, looked at those standing around, and said, "This fellow was also with Jesus of Nazareth." Simon Peter looked at them and again denied the Lord as he swore and said, "I know not the man!" (see Matt. 26:72).

His rough language must have convinced them that he was telling the truth because things calmed down. He struck up a conversation as he stood there trying to blend in with the crowd when he was apparently interrupted. "Hey you, you are one of those who followed Jesus; your speech betrays you" (see Matt. 26:73). Simon Peter became so angry that he began to curse and swear, declaring no connection to Jesus whatsoever. His accusers were now in shock, listening to this Galilaean curse and swear. In the midst of his denunciation he was again interrupted, but this time the sound sent chills through his heart. Peter heard the sound of a cock crowing. He stopped mid-sentence and began to weep.

He had done just as Jesus had said, "Before the cock crows, you will have denied me three times." How could he have denied the Lord? At that moment Jesus was being led out of the hall, and for what seemed like an eternity, their eyes met. He couldn't take it; he had to get out of there. With hot tears flowing down his face, Peter ran. He couldn't believe what he had done. He couldn't stop crying; it seemed that his heart would explode. There in the pre-dawn hours in Jerusalem he cried out to God and repented.

Just as the Lord spoke to me regarding the "Judas Factor" and what would happen in America following the Iran nuclear deal, He also directed me to the parallels between His disciples and the last-day church. Now that it looks like the deal is all but finished and the United States of America has become complicit with the enemies of Israel, where does that leave the body of Christ?

It is easy to become critical of Peter and the other disciples for the way they responded at the hour of the betrayal. How could they betray Christ in His hour of need? How could you celebrate with Him one hour and deny Him the next? In the few short days between the triumphal entry and the crucifixion, the disciples had seen it all. On the one hand, they had witnessed the crowds and dreamed of crowns; and on the other hand, they had watched it all crumble. Their hopes and dreams were no doubt tied to His popularity, and now that was gone.

So many had followed Jesus as long as He was healing and blessing, but now that the crowds were no longer there, it was a different story. Jesus warned them that a time was coming when their faith would be tested and their commitment tried. When the time came, one by one they fled; they turned their back on Christ when He needed them most. They celebrated the popular Jesus, but ran from the crucified Jesus.

The church in America is at a crossroad—we love the crowds, but have rejected the Cross. There are many who have walked with Christ and are now on the fence. It's not that they don't love Him; it's just that they don't want to offend anyone by talking about the Cross. The Cross has become offensive in today's church. Our pulpits are filled with modern-day pillow prophets. We want to be accepted; we want to be popular. Our denominations are led by those who are more focused on crowds and crowns than the Cross. We spend much of our energy preaching the gospel of accommodation and acceptance. We have watered down our sermons and fashioned our "worship" services in such a way to assure the seeker that he or she will never be offended at our churches.

In the Old Testament, God warned the "pillow prophets" in Israel that judgment was coming. He cried out to those who compromised His Word and spoke only of peace and blessing. He said to them, "As the thief is ashamed when he is found, so is the house of Israel ashamed; they, their kings, their princes, and their priests, and their prophets" (Jer. 2:26). I believe God was saying that when this thing begins to shake and judgment begins to fall, all of those who are caught up in the seeker-sensitive movement will be ashamed. Judgment will reveal their compromise. Those to whom they have preached their soft gospel will demand an answer for their lack of willingness to stand with Christ.

The shame that filled Simon Peter as he heard the crowing of the cock is soon to fill the hearts of many ministers of the gospel. There will be many ministers who will recognize their betrayal and do as Peter did; they will fall on their faces in repentance. They will be broken before the Lord, and because of their brokenness, they will be restored.

As the Lord began to reveal this word to my heart, He told me to tread lightly when dealing with the pillow prophets of the modern church because they were His and He would deal with them in His way. I was grieved with the watered-down sermons that were being preached and the lack of willingness of these preachers to take a stand for Christ. My heart broke for the condition of the modern church when God reminded me that the church is His— and that many of the ministers who have denied Him are going to hear the cock crow. There are many others who will continue down the path of destruction; they have ears to hear, but they do not hear. It is for them and their congregations that my heart breaks.

Simon Peter is proof that God can take someone who has denied Him and turn them into a powerhouse for the kingdom of God. God is calling out to us. He desires to put His glory in us and use us to shake this generation. If the church awakens and prays, I believe we will see the greatest outpouring of any generation in history. We should do what Noah did—target our family. I may not get everyone on the ark, but I am going to get my family in. If all of us would do that, we could affect this generation.

While there is a real concern for this generation that desires to purge God from our culture, God has an answer. Noah's ship sailed off through the rising waters with his family safe and protected. Likewise, the church is not destined for the same destruction as the nation. God will take care of us! Although many within the church have gone astray and there is indeed a great falling away, all is not lost. God has a remnant who has not bowed the knee to Baal, and He is about to reveal Himself to those who will hear His call.

What is the answer for these troubled times? It's the same today as it was in the post-resurrection message of Jesus to His disciples: "You shall receive power after that the Holy Ghost has come upon you...don't leave Jerusalem without it!" (see Acts 1:8). The answer to the coming judgment is a church on fire. When God was finished with the disciples, they shook their world. They went in to the upper room in Acts 1 needing power. They went in timid and shy, nervous and scared, but they came out ten days later with the fire of another world burning in their souls.

Peter, who only days earlier had denied Christ, now stood on the balcony of an upper room boldly proclaiming the kingdom of God. Thank God there are some preachers who, even though they have failed God in the past, are about to be turned around. There are some prophets who have been caught up in the crowds and crown movement who are about to experience the fire of God.

Are there difficult days ahead for the church? Yes, there are some very dark days ahead as we watch our nation take sides against Israel. The church will experience a time of sifting and shaking. Many freedoms that we now enjoy may soon be lost, but all that will do is force us to get into our closet of prayer. The more pressure the enemy applies, the more the church will pray, and when the church prays, God responds.

The message of God to the church is this: God is in control, and the church is in His hand. Our responsibility is to stand by the nation of Israel in our prayers and with our support. While our nation is preparing to be shaken like no other nation in history, we must not be. Stand on the Word of God!

By signing a nuclear agreement with Iran, we have sanctioned evil. We have invited the judgment of God upon our land; everything that can be shaken will be shaken. The true church is unshakeable, no weapon formed against it shall prosper, and the gates of hell cannot stop it. When the smoke has cleared and the dust has settled, the church of the Living God will stand.

In the end, only two entities will survive—the nation of Israel and the church. It will not be because America or any other nation has saved her or protected her, but because God Almighty has. In the war of Gog and Magog recorded in Ezekiel 38 and 39, we are told that it will be God alone who protects His chosen people. He also assures us that those who turn against Israel will be destroyed.

As Judas betrayed Christ, America will betray Israel. The end of both will be the same. As Christ was resurrected and continues to reign, Israel has been resurrected and will never be defeated again. The church stands at a crossroad, we will either remain unprepared for the days ahead, or we will find our way to an upper room.

CHAPTER 17

JUDAS AND AMERICA

Life in Post-Christian America

THE PALE, GRAY light had passed into that of early morning, when the Sanhedrin once more assembled in the Palace of Caiaphas. It had been a tragic night to say the least, and now things had taken an even more dramatic turn. There was no way that Judas or any of the others could have imagined what was awaiting them. Everything was spinning out of control. It seemed that with each passing moment a little more of the world they had known just a few hours earlier was coming unhinged.

The disciples had fled just as Jesus said they would. He had warned them that "when the Shepherd was smitten, the sheep would scatter," and that is exactly what happened. Some were hiding out in Jerusalem; some had followed the Master, albeit at a distance. Christ had been bound and led back up the slope to the palace of Annas, and from there He had been rushed to the house of Caiaphas. Morning sun was beginning to break on this "Good Friday," but the darkness that hung over the city was anything but good.

Judas watched as much as he could, but it was all more than he could have imagined. The face that he had kissed was now unrecognizable. It dripped with spit and blood and was already beginning to swell. Even the cruel beating at the whipping post could not satisfy the crowd. They demanded His death, and that is exactly what they would get.

It was then that Judas remembered the bag; he had somehow forgotten it as he was caught up in the excitement of the scene unfolding in front of him. How could thirty pieces of silver weigh so much? At that moment, he realized that it wasn't the weight of the silver that was so heavy but the weight of betrayal. He had no one to blame, and there was no one to point the finger at—he had sold Jesus.

Daylight revealed the darkness that was moving inside of him. What happened to those feelings of power that he felt as he led that riotous crowd to Jesus? What happened to that sense of accomplishment, that satisfaction? All of it was gone. There was nothing left of the euphoria that he felt as he leaned forward to kiss Jesus there in the garden. Betrayal. Its weight was now squarely on the shoulders of Judas.

His mind was reeling; he hadn't slept for days. How long had it been? The betrayal had taken its toll on Judas. It had been a flurry of plotting and planning, scheming and conniving. In his mind he replayed that scene at the house in Bethany. He had rebuked Jesus for letting that woman waste the oil on Him, and there in front of everyone Jesus chastised him. Judas couldn't shake the words Jesus had said, "She has anointed my body for death" (see John 12:7). Had Jesus known what was going on inside of Judas? He was equally haunted by the conversation that occurred as he dipped bread with Jesus just the previous evening: "One of you will betray me!" (see Matt. 26:21).

What had he done? Satan had entered into him, but the devil cannot be fully to blame. This betrayal had certainly been conceived in the mind of Satan, but Judas had been a willing participant in the scheme. Now there was no joy, no elation, no peace. It was all gone. There was nothing but the weight of his actions and the weight of that bag.

He could hear the rattle of the coins with every movement he made. The incessant clanging was enough to drive a man mad. He switched the bag from one hand to the next, but nothing he could do made it any lighter. The silver coins seemed to be louder than the mob that was now screaming for the crucifixion. Judas was being crushed by feelings of remorse and guilt. In an effort to lighten the load that his heart was feeling, he ran out of that judgment hall. He wasn't sure where to go or what to do next, but he knew he had to get out of there. The pounding of his heart and the rattling coins were only matched in intensity by the growing mob that now was screaming, "Crucify, crucify, crucify!" He had reached his breaking point; something had to give. The streets of the city were now busy; it seemed that everyone was rushing toward Pilate's hall, but not Judas. He had to find a way to lighten the load that was now crushing him.

Everywhere he looked he could see Jesus. He could hear Jesus. All of the miracles that he had witnessed were now being played over and over in his mind. That smile, those eyes that were so full of compassion. What had he done? For three-and-a-half years he had walked with Him, and now it was all over. Tears flooded his face as he ran by the steps leading to the temple. Seized with remorse, he now stood in the place where he had been just a few short hours earlier. Judas returned the thirty silver coins to the chief priests and the elders. They had delivered Jesus to Pilate and were trying to get back to their priestly responsibilities when they heard Judas scream, "I have sinned," he said, "for I have betrayed innocent blood." "What is that to us?" they replied. "That's your responsibility" (see Matt. 27:4). So Judas threw the money into the temple and left.

It was not enough. Judas had no one to turn to; he had no money, and no friends. This man from Kerioth had come to the end of the road. His remorse only intensified as he ran from the temple. What happened next is the perfect example of the destruction that awaits those who allow themselves to be used of the devil. Judas hanged himself! What more can be said? What had been done was done. This once-powerful man, this treasurer, this one-time disciple had committed suicide. His name is forever synonymous with betrayal. The torture that Judas went through in those last few hours cannot be fathomed. No book, no movie, and no actor could properly portray the agony of his soul. Judas...

While we can only imagine what it must have felt like to betray Christ, we can more easily describe what it will be like to betray Israel. We are witnessing the meetings with Israel's enemies, and we are watching them march toward the garden. The torches are lighting the night sky as nearer and nearer they come to the place where America will forsake Israel.

American leadership wants so desperately to be post-Christian. Our leaders have done everything in their power to distance our country from its Judeo-Christian heritage. We have legalized everything that God has called evil and made evil everything that God has called good. We have embraced the spirit of Sodom and rejected the Spirit of God. The blood of 56 million babies cries out for justice, but instead of closing the abortion mills, Obamacare now funds them more deeply. The only thing left to do in this awful hour of betrayal is to finalize our offense to God by cursing His chosen people Israel.

When it's all said and done, what will America look like? When the negotiations with Iran have been completed, when we have denigrated the Bible and the principles upon which we were founded, will we be recognizable? We as a nation are teetering on the brink of bankruptcy both financially and morally. It hasn't happened overnight, but it certainly has intensified exponentially over the past seven years under the presidency of Barack Obama. It seems as though he moves with a satanic anointing, doing everything in his power to fundamentally and systematically destroy and dismantle every principle upon which our nation was established.

God has instructed us to bless Israel, and as I stated earlier, He has blessed us because we have been a blessing to them. He also warned us not to curse Israel. He said that He would curse any nation that cursed His people. What does a cursed nation look like? What are the repercussions of a national curse?

THE SUN NEVER SETS ON THE BRITISH EMPIRE

Though the term *empire* never really fit Great Britain in many aspects, that is what they were. In each of the 24 time zones around the world, the kingdom of Great Britain could be found. Their power was unmatched; no nation in the history of the world had ever controlled so much landmass. The sun was indeed shining on a portion of this kingdom every hour of the day. The British military might was unrivaled. One needs only to look at a map of their worldwide dominion and of the nations that were under their control to understand the power of that statement. In less than 100 years, this once-mighty nation who boasted of so much power now stands as a warning to America of what can happen when you mishandle God's chosen people.

The great writer, Rudyard Kipling penned the "Recessional" in 1897, and it serves as a warning to America today:

> God of our fathers, known of old,
>   Lord of our far-flung battle-line,
> Beneath whose awful Hand we hold
>   Dominion over palm and pine—
> Lord God of Hosts, be with us yet,
>   Lest we forget—lest we forget!
>
> The tumult and the shouting dies;
>   The Captains and the Kings depart:
> Still stands Thine ancient sacrifice,
>   An humble and a contrite heart.
> Lord God of Hosts, be with us yet,
>   Lest we forget—lest we forget!
>
> Far-called, our navies melt away;
>   On dune and headland sinks the fire:
> Lo, all our pomp of yesterday
>   Is one with Nineveh and Tyre!
> Judge of the Nations, spare us yet,
>   Lest we forget—lest we forget!
>
> If, drunk with sight of power, we loose
>   Wild tongues that have not Thee in awe,
> Such boastings as the Gentiles use,
>   Or lesser breeds without the Law—
> Lord God of Hosts, be with us yet,
>   Lest we forget—lest we forget!

For heathen heart that puts her trust
  In reeking tube and iron shard,
All valiant dust that builds on dust,
  And guarding, calls not Thee to guard,
For frantic boast and foolish word—
  Thy mercy on Thy People, Lord![1]

The poem is a prayer. It describes two fates that befall even the most powerful people, armies, and nations, and that threatened England at the time: passing out of existence and lapsing from Christian faith into profanity. The prayer entreats God to spare England from these fates "lest we forget" the sacrifice of Christ.

Today the greatness of Britain is long gone. This once-great nation upon which the "sun never set" is now overtaken by wickedness and perversion. The landmass they once boasted of is no more. They now stand as a nation among nations as the sun has now begun to set. If the trends continue, in just a few short years Islam will become the predominant religion of this once-Christian nation. The words that were written so long ago by Rudyard Kipling went unheeded.

It was at the pinnacle of their worldwide influence from 1919 to 1942 that Great Britain began to lose its greatness. What caused them to unravel? It was their treatment of the Jews. Although in control of the territory known as Palestine, Great Britain announced in the 1939 "White Paper" that an independent Arab state would be created within ten years, and that Jewish immigration was to be limited to 75,000 for the next five years, after which it was to cease altogether. It also forbade land sales to Jews in 95 percent of the territory of Palestine.

The British Empire was effectively denying the people of Israel the right to exist in the land that God had given them. Furthermore, while the Jews were being slaughtered by Nazi Germany, Great Britain closed its borders and the borders to its territories to the Jewish people. As a result of their actions, hundreds of thousands of God's people were stranded in Europe where they were rounded up like animals and slaughtered in Hitler's death camps. They missed their opportunity to stand on the right side of history—and more importantly, on the right side of God. They failed to see what God was doing at this time in history. There was a new wind blowing, and God was in the process of bringing His scattered sheep home again.

> That then the LORD thy God will turn thy captivity, and have compassion upon thee, and will return and gather thee from all the nations, whither the LORD thy God hath scattered thee.
> —DEUTERONOMY 30:3

> Hear the word of the LORD, O ye nations, and declare it in the isles afar off, and say, He that scattered Israel will gather him, and keep him, as a shepherd doth his flock.
> —JEREMIAH 31:10

> Therefore say, Thus saith the Lord GOD; I will even gather you from the people, and assemble you out of the countries where ye have been scattered, and I will give you the land of Israel.
> —EZEKIEL 11:17

> And I scattered them among the heathen, and they were dispersed through the countries: according to

their way and according to their doings I judged
them.

—Ezekiel 36:19

The time of the dispersion of the Jewish people was
coming to an end. Unfortunately, Great Britain, who
might have been a major player in the plan of God, would
instead become an obstacle. They missed their greatest
moment in history. God had positioned them as the care-
takers of Zion, and they let it slip through their hands.
From that time forward, you can mark the decline of this
once-great nation.

Is the same fate awaiting America? Are we so foolish as
to think that the same cannot happen to us? We have not
risen to this place of power and prestige, but for the grace
of God. Why has He put us in power? Why has God been
so gracious to America? Because of our covenant with
Him and our covenant with Israel, we have been blessed
above all nations in the world, and yet we are systematically breaking each of these covenants.

Why hasn't God judged America already? I would argue
that He has. I believe we have witnessed many judgments
throughout the past few years. To understand God's ways
you have to understand His Word. He still operates within
the framework of the Bible. If you want to know how
He moves now, you only need to look at how He moved
then. Amos 4 shows us God's means and methods as He
attempted to turn Israel around. There are six areas that
were impacted as God sought to turn them back:

Great out of or food stamps 2016

1. Lack of food—hunger

And I also have given you cleanness of teeth in all your cities, and want of bread in all your places: yet have ye not returned unto me, saith the LORD.

—Amos 4:6

Happening Today 2016

2. Rain—crazy weather patterns

lack of in California

And also I have withholden the rain from you, when there were yet three months to the harvest: and I caused it to rain upon one city, and caused it not to rain upon another city: one piece was rained upon, and the piece whereupon it rained not withered.

flooding in midwest

—Amos 4:7

many cities sell water to another

3. Dissatisfaction—the continual search

Bethalto Buys alton water

So two or three cities wandered unto one city, to drink water; but they were not satisfied: yet have ye not returned unto me, saith the LORD.

—Amos 4:8

4. Heat waves and drought

Georgia Florida Texas

I have smitten you with blasting [blight caused by heat] and mildew [caused by drought]: when your gardens and your vineyards and your fig trees and your olive trees increased, the palmerworm devoured them: yet have ye not returned unto me, saith the LORD.

—Amos 4:9

crop failures

5. Pestilence

defeat in Vietnam

I have sent among you the pestilence after the manner of Egypt: your young men have I slain with the sword, and have taken away your horses; and

I have made the stink of your camps to come up
unto your nostrils: yet have ye not returned unto
me, saith the LORD.

—Amos 4:10

6. Judgment on immorality

I have overthrown some of you, as God overthrew
Sodom and Gomorrah, and ye were as a firebrand
plucked out of the burning: yet have ye not returned
unto me, saith the LORD.

—Amos 4:11

moral failures by many

What followed should cause great trepidation for
America. God said to Israel, "You haven't returned to
Me despite all of these warnings, so "prepare to meet
thy God!"

He shouts out to us in verse 13, "I brought you into existence and I can take you out. I raised you up and I can
pull you down. I am God!"

For, lo, he that formeth the mountains, and crea-
teth the wind, and declareth unto man what is his
thought, that maketh the morning darkness, and
treadeth upon the high places of the earth, The
LORD, The God of hosts, is his name.

—Amos 4:13

In 1893, Katharine Lee Bates penned the first version of
these beautiful words to describe the majesty and beauty
of the United States of America:

O beautiful for spacious skies,
For amber waves of grain,
For purple mountain majesties
Above the fruited plain!

209

America! America!
  God shed his grace on thee
And crown thy good with brotherhood
  From sea to shining sea!

O beautiful for pilgrim feet
  Whose stern impassioned stress
A thoroughfare of freedom beat
  Across the wilderness!

America! America!
  God mend thine every flaw,
Confirm thy soul in self-control,
  Thy liberty in law![2]

God has given us ample warnings. He is trying to turn us back to Himself. God loves America, but America now stands with the rope in our hands; like Judas, our next move could hang us.

A BLESSED LAND OR A CURSED LAND

To fully grasp what God's blessings can do for a country, just take a look at modern Israel. In Isaiah 27:6, God said Israel's fruit would fill the world. The prophet says that Israel would one day blossom and fill the world with its fruit. This prophecy has been fulfilled. Today, the land of Israel, which had been barren for centuries, is a leading producer of agricultural products, exporting food to many countries. All of this is a far cry from the situation a century ago. When Jews began resettling their historic homeland in the late nineteenth century, their first efforts were directed toward reclaiming the mostly semi-arid land, much of which was rendered untillable by deforestation, soil erosion, and neglect. Rocky fields were cleared and

210

terraces built in the hilly regions; swampland was drained, and systematic reforestation begun; soil erosion was counteracted, and salty land washed to reduce soil salinity. Israel's varied climatic, topographical, and soil conditions (from sub-tropical to arid; from 400 meters below sea level to 1000 meters above; and from sand dunes to heavy alluvial soils) made it possible to grow a wide range of agricultural produce.

In Isaiah 41:18–20, God said that the trees would grow again in Israel. The Prophet Isaiah said that during the restoration of Israel the construction of a vast irrigation system would improve farming. The lack of available water, including rain, is one reason why Israel had been a desolate, unproductive land during much of the past 2000 years. During the 1900s, when many Jews returned to their ancient homeland, they fulfilled Isaiah's prophecy and built a network of irrigation systems. Over the past century, more than 200 million trees have been planted in Israel.

In Isaiah 51, God promised that Israel's deserts will become like the "Garden of Eden." On a recent trip to Israel I witnessed the fulfillment of this great prophecy. The Jews have been irrigating, cultivating, and reconditioning the land—and as a result, many of the country's swamps, which had been infested with malaria, have been converted into farmland. And water from the Sea of Galilee has been channeled through portions of the deserts, allowing some of the deserts to bloom. Israel is now a food source for many countries.

In the land of milk and honey, water has always been in short supply, until now. In July of 2015, an Israeli desalination firm was named one of the world's smartest companies as reported by *Jerusalem Post*.[3] The country that was once a desert is now experiencing a water surplus.

> The wilderness and the solitary place shall be glad for them; and the desert shall rejoice, and blossom as the rose.
>
> —ISAIAH 35:1

What has caused this turnaround in the nation of Israel? While some would argue that it has been through the efforts of brilliant people, I would suggest that it is the blessing of God. There are brilliant people in many barren lands.

The first 13 verses of Deuteronomy 28 tell us of all of the blessings that will rest upon a nation that joins in covenant with God. These are blessings that have rested upon our nation until recent years. Twenty-one blessings are promised to those who walk in covenant with God:

1. God will set you "on high above all the other nations of the earth: and all these blessings shall come on you, and overtake you" (Deut. 28:1–2).

2. You will be blessed in the city (Deut. 28:3).

3. You will be blessed in the field (Deut. 28:3).

4. You will have perfect offspring (Deut. 28:4).

5. Your crops will be blessed (Deut. 28:4).

6. Your cattle will increase (Deut. 28:4).

7. Your flocks will increase (Deut. 28:4).

8. Your baskets and storehouses will be full of good things (Deut. 28:5, 8).

9. You will be blessed in all you undertake (Deut. 28:6, 8).

10. You will have complete victory over all your enemies (Deut. 28:7).

11. Your land will be abundantly fertile and productive (Deut. 28:8).

12. You will be established as a holy people to God (Deut. 28:9).

13. You will be a witness and an example to all people on earth (Deut. 28:10).

14. All nations will be afraid of you (Deut. 28:10).

15. You will be prosperous in goods, in children, in stock, and in crops in all the land (Deut. 28:11).

16. The Lord will open to you all His good treasure (Deut. 28:12).

17. The heavens will give you rain in due season in all your land (Deut. 28:12).

18. The Lord will bless all the work of your hands (Deut. 28:12).

19. You will be prosperous enough to lend to many nations, and you will not need to borrow from them (Deut. 28:12).

20. The Lord shall make you the head, and not the tail (Deut. 28:13).

21. You shall be above all men and never beneath them (Deut. 28:13).

It is interesting to note that America never lost a war until 1973 when we withdrew our troops from Vietnam. It was the same year that we legalized the slaughter of unborn babies. We broke covenant with God; now we are experiencing the signs of a nation under a curse. Look at what the Bible says will happen to a nation when God's blessings are removed:

1. Pestilence cleaving to you (Deut. 28:21–22)

2. Death or being consumed off the land (Deut. 28:20)

3. Consumption (Deut. 28:22; Lev. 26:16)

4. Fever (Deut. 28:22; Lev. 26:16)

5. Inflammation (Deut. 28:22)

6. Extreme burning (Deut. 28:22)

7. Sword (Deut. 28:22; Lev. 26:17, 25, 42)

8. Blasting (Deut. 28:22; Lev. 26:18–20)

9. Mildew (Deut. 28:22)

10. The sky like brass (Deut. 28:23; Lev. 26:19)

11. The ground like iron (Deut. 28:23; Lev. 26:20)

12. Drought, dust—no rain (Deut. 28:24)

13. Destruction because of long drought (Deut. 28:24)

14. Smitten before enemies (Deut. 28:25; Lev. 26:17–39)

15. Going out one way, fleeing seven ways (Deut. 28:25)

16. Dispersion into all kingdoms of the earth (Deut. 28:25)

17. Bodies eaten by fowls and beasts (Deut. 28:26)

18. The plagues of Egypt (Deut. 28:27)

19. Emerods (Deut. 28:27)

20. Scab (Deut. 28:27)

21. Itch (Deut. 28:27)

22. Diseases with no cure (Deut. 28:27)

23. Madness (Deut. 28:28)

24. Blindness (Deut. 28:28)

25. Astonishment of heart (Deut. 28:28)

26. Groping at noonday (Deut. 28:29)

27. No prosperity (Deut. 28:29)

28. Oppressed and spoiled forever (Deut. 28:29)

29. No man to save you (Deut. 28:29)

If you want to see how dangerous it is to fight God, study the entirety of the 28th chapter of Deuteronomy. My heart grieves to think of the curses that loom ahead. We cannot afford to have God remove His hand of favor from our land. God has promised us that the healing of our land can happen, but it is contingent upon our willingness to pray and repent. Israel is a perfect picture of what healed land can look like.

LIVING UNDER THE CURSE

God told Adam that the ground was under a curse because of his rebellion. That curse hindered everything that Adam would do from that moment forward. Furthermore, when God cursed Cain for murdering his brother Abel, part of that curse included the ground. The cities of Sodom and Gomorrah, Tyre and Sidon, all experienced the swift judgment of God. The land there is cursed because of their wickedness.

There is a great scripture that so many are clinging to and believing today; it is 2 Chronicles 7:14. In it, God promises healing for the land if the conditions are met. While many gravitate to this text and its promise, they bypass what the land looks like while it is being cursed. When a land is cursed, there are often a series of events that open the door to destruction. God is warning Israel of three things that happen. He says, "If I shut up heaven that there be no rain, or if I command the locusts to devour the land, or if I send pestilence among my people" (2 Chron. 7:13).

1. Heaven either produces no rain, or as we have seen in previous scriptures, crazy rain patterns. Unpredictable weather patterns are now beginning to take place. This is not produced by man-made carbon gasses as the socialists and globalists would like to make

216

you believe. They are signs of the judgment of God being unleashed on the Earth.

2. God commands a devouring of the land. Things will begin to happen that eat up or consume the land.

According to *Vine's Expository Dictionary of Old Testament and New Testament Words,* the word for pestilence is *deber* and can mean "death or misfortune."[4] The word occurs fewer than 60 times in the Old Testament, and mainly in the prophets Jeremiah and Ezekiel. The meaning of *deber* is best denoted by the English word *pestilence* or *plague.* A country might be quickly reduced in population by the plague (see 2 Sam. 24:13 ff.). The nature of the plague is often difficult to determine from the contexts, as the details of medical interest are not given or are scanty. In the prophetic writings, the plague occurs with other disasters: famine, flood, and the sword: "When they fast, I will not hear their cry; and when they offer burnt offering and an oblation, I will not accept them: but I will consume them by the sword, and by the famine, and by the pestilence" (Jer. 14:12).

Is America going to face the judgment of God described in these verses? Some would suggest that we are already seeing many of them unfold. Will America experience the healing that we so desperately need or the judgment that God has warned us of? There is still hope! It doesn't take an army to turn the nation? One man or woman and God is enough to turn a nation. He used Jonah to turn Nineveh to repentance. God raised up Gideon to bring victory to Israel, and even though his numbers were small, he did great and mighty things. Where are the "Jonahs" and the

"Gideons"? Where are the prophets? The Lord spoke to Elijah in the cave and told him there were 7000 prophets alive in the land who had not bowed the knee to Baal. If God could reserve 7000 out of the tribes of Israel, then I am convinced that He has a remnant who will hear His call and help turn this nation before it's too late.

> If my people, which are called by my name, shall humble themselves, and pray, and seek my face, and turn from their wicked ways; then will I hear from heaven, and will forgive their sin, and will heal their land.
>
> —2 CHRONICLES 7:14

I don't know all that lies ahead, but I know that God is in charge. The church is not without hope! God has us in the palm of His hand, and He has promised to be faithful to us. We must repent and return to our first love. We must find a secret place with Him where we die out to selfish ambition and self-centered desires for "crowds and crowns." When we do, we will come out of hiding and walk in the power of God. We will see a repairing of the breach, and we will be restorers of His path. We will see many modern-day pillow prophets humbled and repent before God. We will also see many others who will continue to go down the road of betrayal.

God will raise the church out of the ashes. As He said through His Prophet Joel and again through Peter on the Day of Pentecost, "I will pour out My Spirit in those days!" (Joel 2:29; Acts 2:18, NKJV). No one and nothing can stop Him. It is time for you and me to decide whose side we are on. I would rather stand with a lonely Jesus than with a crowd of betrayers, and I would rather see America aligned with Israel than to see us stand shoulder-to-shoulder with those who would attempt to annihilate them.

It's Friday, but Sunday is coming! Jesus arose triumphant, and so will Israel. The Lord who watches over them neither slumbers nor sleeps. May God bless Israel, and may He save America!

ENDNOTES

1.   Rudyard Kipling, "Recessional," *A Choice of Kipling's Verse* (London: Faber and Faber, 1943).

2.   Katherine Lee Bates, "America the Beautiful" (1893), public domain.

3.   Yoram Gabison, Inbal Orpaz, and TheMarker, "Tech-Nation Israeli Desalination Company Named among World's 50 'Smartest Firms,'" Haaretz, July 7, 2015, http://www.haaretz.com /business/tech-roundup/.premium-1.664685.

4.   W.E. Vine, Merrill Unger, and William White, *Vine's Complete Expository Dictionary of Old and New Testament Words* (Nashville: T. Nelson, 1996).

ABOUT THE AUTHOR

DWIGHT JONES IS the Senior Pastor of Harvest Christian Centre (Assemblies of God) in Park Hills, MO. He and Tammy, his wife of nearly 30 years, have three daughters and three grandchildren. In addition to pastoring a church with more than 1200 attendees, Dwight travels extensively preaching revivals and prophecy conferences as well as national and international conferences and camps.

CONTACT THE AUTHOR

FOR MORE INFORMATION on the ministry of Pastor Dwight Jones, please visit him at reapnow.org or DwightJonesMinistries.org. You can also join people from more than 30 countries worldwide who watch the Reapnow broadcast on Roku or on the web at reapnow.org. For booking information or to contact Dwight, please call 573-431-3266.